An Accurate MAP of the WEST INDIES.

Exhibiting not only all the Islands possess'd by the English, French, Spaniards & Dutch, but also all the Towns and Settlements on the Continent of America adjacent thereto.

K. Charles II. by Charter dated June 30 1665 granted to L.d Chanc.r Clarendon, D. of Albemarle, &c. the Province of Carolina extending Southward to the 29. Deg. of. North Lat. which takes in F. S.t Augustin now possessed by the Spaniards; — In 1729 the British Parliament purchased S. Carolina of the Proprietors for his Majesty K. George II. who soon after granted to Trustees for establishing y.e Colony of Georgia the Lands between the Rivers Savannah and Alatamaha

The Spanish Gallions coming before R. de la Hacha notice is sent thither & from thence over land to Cartagena, Lima, Panama &c. to hasten the King's Treasure. They then continue their Course to Cartagena and after a stay of 2 Months go to Puerto Bello and are about a Month taking in the Treasure from Panama &c. then they return to Cartagena finish their Lading & Sail to the Havana to meet the Flota from la Vera Crux, whence they proceed together thro the Gulf of Florida for Old Spain.

Bermudas I.

FROM Jamaica to the W. Point of Cuba
From the W.t Point of Jamaica to the W. Point of Cuba Ships have the advantage of the Trade Winds, which are for that till they get into the Gulph as much against them; so that while they are trying it between Cape Florida and Cuba, the Guarda Costas from the latter can easily bear down upon them. Again, as the Florida Coast is flat and Shoaly for 7 or 8. Leagues out they are obliged to keep near the Bahamas, and are again in danger from thence, all those Islands being Spanish, except Providence, where if our Ships get, and take any Logwood on board, tho' the Growth of that Island, the Spanish Guarda Costas which lie of the Abaco I. will make Prize of them pretending that Wood only grows in their Territories.

FROM Jamaica by the Windward Passage.
The most difficult part of this Course is from Port Royal to Point Morant which being against y.e Trade Winds, has sometimes taken up 6 Weeks, tho' but 20 Leagues. But the most dangerous is from that Point till they are clear of Crooked Island, a Course of 160 Leag. for the Spaniards from Cuba, Porto Rico & Hispaniola (and sometimes the French) are in wait to intercept y.e English This is called the Windward Passage because Ships are obliged to keep to the Windward to avoid the Shoals on the Coast of Cuba.

A T L A N T I C K

In 1700 the Bahama Islands which belong'd to the English were taken by the French & Spaniards; In 1717 Captain Rogers after having plunder'd most of those Islands retreck Providence which has ever since belong'd to y.e English.

W E S T E R N

O C E A N

A Scale of Leagues 20 to a Degree

C A R I B E E I S L A N D S

HISPANIOLA

P.to Rico

JAMAICA

Antilles Islands

N O R T H   S E A

Great

Lit. Antilles Islands

Barbadoes

S.t Lucia

Martinica

Guadaloupe

Dominica

Tobago

Granada

Trinidad

Oronoque Islands
Oronoque R.

NEW GRANADA, S.t FE

OR

CASTILLA DEL ORO

VENEZUELA

ANDALUZIA

T E R R A   F I R M A

SURINAM

CARACOS

C. Charles
C. Henry
Albemarle Sound
Roanoke Inlet
Cape Hatteras
Cape Look out

Chesapeak

Long I.
Cat I.
Watlings

Crooked I.
Mayaguana I.
Caicos Bank

Tortuga I.

THE
PUNCH
BOWL

To Kristin

STERLING EPICURE
New York

An Imprint of Sterling Publishing
387 Park Avenue South
New York, NY 10016

10 9 8 7 6 5 4 3 2 1

Published by Sterling Publishing Co., Inc.
387 Park Avenue South, New York, NY 10016
© 2011 by Dan Searing
Distributed in Canada by Sterling Publishing
c/o Canadian Manda Group, 165 Dufferin Street
Toronto, Ontario, Canada M6K 3H6
Distributed in the United Kingdom by GMC Distribution Services
Castle Place, 166 High Street, Lewes, East Sussex, England BN7 1XU
Distributed in Australia by Capricorn Link (Australia) Pty. Ltd.
P.O. Box 704, Windsor, NSW 2756, Australia

Printed in China

Cover and book design by Laurie Dolphin and Allison Meierding
Edited by Jessica Jones
Concept by Jessica Jones
Cocktail photography by Ken Skalski
Punch bowl photography by Stuart S. Shapiro
Still-life photography by Mark A. Gore
Produced by Dolphin + Jones Book Packaging and Media

Sterling ISBN 978-1-4027-8582-5

For information about custom editions, special sales, premium and corporate purchases, please contact Sterling Special Sales Department at 800-805-5489 or specialsales@sterlingpublishing.com.

PRODUCED BY
dolphin + jones

THE
PUNCH
BOWL

75 Recipes Spanning Four Centuries of Wanton Revelry

DAN SEARING

STERLING EPICURE
New York

CONTENTS

PART I

THE WORLD OF PUNCH

INTRODUCTION

AS A YOUNG CHILD, I would often stare at my parents' collection of nineteenth- and early-twentieth-century punch-bowl sets and wonder what sort of punch could possibly warrant a grand piece of decorated porcelain, an extravagant cut-glass bowl, or a grand silver ladle. It was only many years later, upon entering the world of wine and spirits, that I learned just how worthy the most classic of punches are of an extraordinary presentation.

Through my work in the world of high-end liquor importing, I've had the good fortune to learn about traditional punches from the historian and noted author David Wondrich, who taught me that in its golden era, punch embodied all things exotic and expensive: spice, sugar, fruit, imported spirits, and, if the imbibers were truly fortunate, clean water. It should come as no surprise that gilded porcelain, silver, and even gold punch bowls (and equally elaborate ladles) were produced for its service. Many nineteenth-century cocktail recipe books would even place the recipes for punches in the front of the volume, thus suggesting their pride of place.

But all this sparkle and grandeur doesn't mean an exceptional punch is out of reach for the average or novice home entertainer. Many traditional recipes, as you'll find throughout this book, are surprisingly easy to prepare. Though some of the ingredients require some leg work to track down, and a few punches need some prep just before service, classic punches are a great way to display your heirlooms and treat guests to something they may not have experienced before. Needless to say, the punches here are dramatically tastier than what you may have sampled at high school or college parties. Forget those grain alcohol concoctions and the sugary Kool-Aid mixtures and enter the realm of the sophisticated (and delicious) punch.

When entertaining my own guests with classic punches, they often comment on the exceptional flavors and aromatics of fruit and spice. Sometimes they even ask to see the ingredients. These experiences while entertaining my friends and colleagues have given me opportunities to showcase not only the classic punches I like best, but also some of the beautiful spirits bottles that have histories just as intriguing as the punch.

Opposite: DOULTON BURSLEM AESTHETIC MOVEMENT TALL FOOTED PUNCH BOWL (C. 1890), *brown transfer decoration and hand-painted highlights of pink and yellow.* Above: 1. PAIRPOINT SILVER PLATED LADLE (C. 1890), *with lobe-shaped bowl and "Aesthetic Movement" repoussé handle with acanthus leaves and floral decoration.* 2. SILVER PLATE PUNCH LADLE (C. 1920S), *with elaborately shaped cup and sterling silver handle.* 3. ROGERS BROTHERS NEO-CLASSICAL SILVER PLATE PUNCH LADLE (C. 1910), *with barley-twist stem and helmet-shaped bowl.* 4. J. B. AND S. M. KNOWLES STERLING SILVER ART NOUVEAU LADLE (C. 1900), *with elaborate scrolling, lobed bowl with gold wash interior.*

The revival of punch is a cornerstone in the reemergence of some long-forgotten traditional spirits. Some are renowned classics, while other spirits are less familiar to the average consumer. Two of the spirits my firm has reintroduced into the U.S. market, with the encouragement of Mr. Wondrich, are: Batavia arrack and pure pot-still Jamaica rum. Batavia arrack, a beguiling and aromatic cane spirits from the East Indies (now Indonesia), became famous in England and the United States for its role as the quintessential spirit for punches. The other more recent introduction is that of old-school, pure pot-still Jamaica rum, made famous in the late nineteenth and early twentieth centuries, when the British still lorded over the islands. Pot-distilling produced a style of rum that gave extraordinarily complex flavor and gravitas to punches and other mixed drinks. Thanks to the resurgence of interest in classic cocktails and punches, there are better spirit selections available today than there have been for decades, making many of the famous punch recipes featured here accessible again.

> ～ **Thanks to the resurgence of interest in classic cocktails and punches, there are better spirit selections available today than there have been for decades**

Whether in premier cocktail bars, restaurants, or at home, it's a joy to see how punch and the elegant bowls from which it is served offer convivial sophistication and efficiency. To the host, a punch prepared in advance affords more time with guests. To the guest, punch offers flavorful complexity and a visual spectacle. By contrast, the straight pour of wines and spirits can seem limiting. A group sharing the same drink has a focal point, a unifying element. Moreover, when serving just a single bowl, an exquisite and exotic aroma can fill a room, leading all present to consider its artful presentation, storied past, and, most especially, its deliciousness. Such is the effect of these punches, and so may it also be for you and your guests.

—Eric Seed

LOBMEYR HAND-BLOWN AUSTRIAN CRYSTAL FOOTED AND COVERED PUNCH BOWL (C. 1890),
With hand-painted, two-color, raised-paste gold grapes and leaves and matching punch cups

MODERNIZING RECIPES

MOST OF THE PUNCHES IN THIS BOOK were developed before the twentieth century, and most of the measurements and instructions used in the original recipes are either incredibly arcane or so brief as to be mystifying. More often than not, the only instructions provided were "Mix well and sweeten to taste." Since many of these punches were made to serve army regiments and other large groups, of one hundred people or more, the recipes sometimes sport phrases like "mix with a wooden paddle" or "place in a trough to serve." Though everyone enjoys a large party, gatherings these days are on a smaller scale, and the usefulness of an oar in stirring libations is questionable. Consequently, the recipes included here have been cut down to a manageable size, the measurements modernized, and the instructions recast in a manner that doesn't require the home bartender to have preexisting knowledge of the subject.

In order to demonstrate how far recipe writing has come, one of the original recipes appears here. Also included is a pre-twentieth-century table of apothecaries' weights and measures and avoirdupois equivalents.

SIGNED LOBMEYR FOOTED CRYSTAL PUNCH CUP (c. 1890), *hand-blown with hand-painted enamel decoration, Austria*

REGENT'S PUNCH

Bottle of sparkling champagne, bottle of hock, gill of dry sherry, gill of pale brandy, ½ gill of rum, gill of lemon-juice, ½ gill of Curaçao, quart of green test, bottle of seltzer water; sugar to taste; ice to the utmost.

See page 147 for the modernized recipe.

APOTHECARIES' MEASURES

Thimbleful	30 drops
Teaspoonful	60 drops
Dessert-spoonful	2 fluid drachms*
Tablespoonful	4 fluid drachms (½ ounce; 1 tablespoon)
Wine-glassful	2 fluid ounces (⅛ of a wine-pint)
Tumblerful	8 fluid ounces (½ pint; 1 cup)
4 gills, or noggins	1 pint (2 cups)
2 pints	1 quart (4 cups)
4 quarts	1 gallon
63 gallons	1 hogshead
84 gallons	1 puncheon

APOTHECARIES' WEIGHT

20 grains	1 scruple
3 scruples	1 drachm
8 drachms	1 ounce (2 tablespoons)
12 ounces	1 pound

AVOIRDUPOIS WEIGHT

16 drachms	1 ounce (2 tablespoons)
16 ounces	1 pound
Pinch of herbs	1 drachm
Handful	10 drachms

*The archaic form of dram

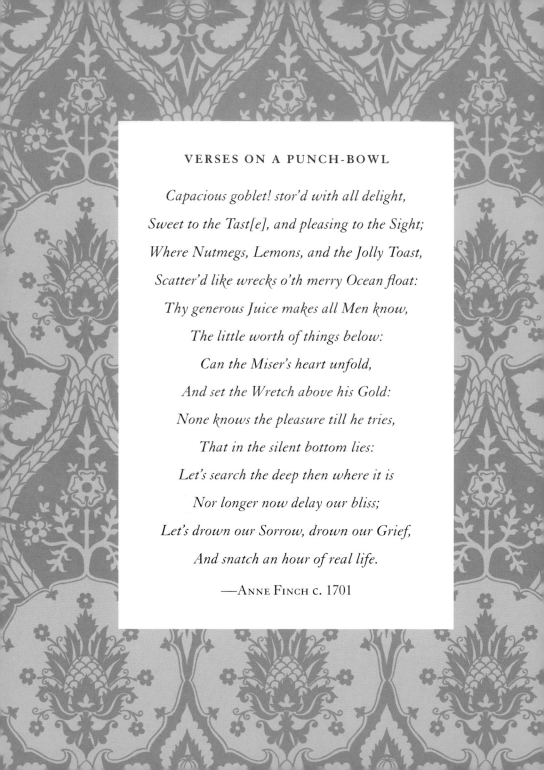

VERSES ON A PUNCH-BOWL

Capacious goblet! stor'd with all delight,
Sweet to the Tast[e], and pleasing to the Sight;
Where Nutmegs, Lemons, and the Jolly Toast,
Scatter'd like wrecks o'th merry Ocean float:
Thy generous Juice makes all Men know,
The little worth of things below:
Can the Miser's heart unfold,
And set the Wretch above his Gold:
None knows the pleasure till he tries,
That in the silent bottom lies:
Let's search the deep then where it is
Nor longer now delay our bliss;
Let's drown our Sorrow, drown our Grief,
And snatch an hour of real life.

—ANNE FINCH c. 1701

THE HISTORY
OF PUNCH

WHILE IT'S A GIVEN that the delights of a well-made punch are numerous, and certainly intoxicating, let's take Anne Finch's lead and remember that the punch bowl itself is an object as worthy of our appreciation as the libation it holds.

Without question, the image of the punch bowl has sunk a few notches since Anne Finch's time. When Finch wrote her tribute to the punch bowl, the drink was extremely popular, having infiltrated the West over the previous century thanks to a combination of improved distillation techniques and the flourishing of trade routes to India and the islands of the Caribbean. (In fact, *punch* is derived from a Hindustani word meaning "five," for the brew's five essential elements: sweet, sour, water, spice, and alcohol.) Sailors on all manner of vessels plying the waters of the Atlantic became particularly fond of the stuff, which quickly found its way into pubs in England and North America, and from there into people's homes. By the nineteenth century, punch was ubiquitous in the West, whether at sea or on dry land.

By the 1950s, the punch bowl—filled with juice and frequently spiked by some kid who had managed to get into his parents' liquor cabinet—had become a workaday vessel doing yeoman's service at corporate parties, school dances, and family rec-room gatherings. Ask anyone today what comes to mind at the mention of the words "punch

bowl" and the answer will likely be a cut-glass or plastic bowl of modest proportions (possibly with matching cups), brimming with a fruity, sticky-sweet concoction of artificial fruit juices in hues of bright red or orange, fortified with a liberal quantity of grain alcohol. Or worse, overflowing with potato chips! Happily, punch is making a comeback as part of the twenty-first-century cocktail renaissance, and for good reason: made with care, it is the ultimate drink to serve at a party (in no small part because it frees up the host to fully participate).

If the same question about the punch bowl's associations were asked of someone alive from the 1700s through the 1800s, a very different answer would have been forthcoming. The image of the punch bowl conjured up

Page 15: Hand-Blown White-Covered Bristol Glass from "Tom & Jerry" Set (c. 1870), *hand-painted raised enamel decoration.* Opposite: Chrysler girls drinking in Detroit, Michigan, 1942. *A footed glass punch bowl keeps spirits up at a corporate party.* Above: "An accurate map of the West Indies" (c. 1752). *Originating in the West Indies in connection with the infamous "triangular trade," rum played a significant role in the evolution of punch.*

Above: "The Catch Singers" (c. 1775), probably by Robert Sayer. *A "catch" was a kind of song born of boisterous (read: bawdy and drunken) conversation, "sung" by three parts. J. Stafford Smith (left) was a member of the Catch Club and, later, of the Royal Anacreontic Society.* Opposite: "Bringing in the Wassail Bowl" (1874), by Henry Stacy Marks. *Wassail is a spiced punch served hot and is especially popular during the holiday season. It originated with the early Saxons.*

for a partygoer or -thrower from this era would be of a highly regarded family heirloom at the heart of large gatherings of revelers as well as intimate family affairs.

One early printed mention of punch and its companion, the punch bowl, appeared in 1672 in *Fryer's Travels*, a popular travelogue of its day. In its pages lies a description of "an enervating liquor, drunk on the [ship known as the] *Coromandel Coast* and deriving its name from the Industani word *paunch*, signifying five; the number of ingredients required to form the mixture." In 1675, the naval chaplain Henry Teonge recorded his first sips of punch, directly from the bowl, which soon became a guzzle-fest during which he

consumed three bowls of the potent mixture on his own. Not surprisingly, Mr. Teonge was worse for wear after his first forays into the unfamiliar world of punch. As punch migrated from India to the West aboard ships like the *Coromandel Coast* and the *Assistance,* more and more people, particularly the English and later the Americans, found that they couldn't get enough of the stuff.

Rum became the likeliest alcohol found in punches of the age of the triangular trade because it is distilled from sugar (molasses, in fact), the principal export item from the Caribbean. Sailors were given alcohol rations (both to induce them to sign on and then to pacify them during long journeys), but spirits were also added to drinking water aboard ocean-crossing vessels to prevent the water from growing algae and becoming non-potable. For all of alcohol's many good uses, ship captains made sure to keep a sizeable supply on board.

> **Rum became the likeliest alcohol found in punches of the age of the triangular trade**

At first, the British Royal Navy favored French brandy for sailors' rations, but that changed after the capture of the island of Jamaica, when the British fleet was introduced to the liquid called "kill-devil" or "rumbullion." Rum, in short. (In fact, rum rations for sailors of the British and Canadian navies continued until July 31, 1970, a date known ruefully thereafter as "Black Tot Day.") In 1740, Vice-Admiral Edward Vernon ordered his sailors' rum rations diluted with a mixture of water and lime or lemon juice (a practice proven seven years later to help prevent that scourge of sailors, scurvy). The popular combination of those three ingredients (known as "grog," in honor of Vernon's trademark grogram coat) got sailors three-fifths of the way to bona fide punch—all that was missing was sugar and, finally, a little spice.

Pirates also enjoyed their booze and likewise used it to maintain order and keep happiness alive aboard ship. Like their counterparts on navy, merchant, and privateer vessels, pirate ships were rife with drunkenness (which was okay, because if liquor wasn't available, even worse mayhem, like mutiny, might ensue). Even a figure as terrifying as the pirate Blackbeard purportedly lamented in his journal his alcohol-related management challenges:

> *Such a day; rum all out. Our company somewhat sober; a damned confusion amongst us! Rogues a plotting. Talk of separation. So I looked sharp for a prize [and] took one with a great deal of liquor aboard. So kept the company hot, damned hot, then all things went well again.*

"Economy" (1816), by George Cruikshank. *Regency-era policies, which included profligate spending by the Prince Regent himself, were evidently discussed over punch.*

When the formula for punch was introduced from India to England, it didn't take long before it jumped from ship to shore. And as love for punch grew, so did the creativity in designing the bowls that would serve this immensely popular beverage.

Punch bowls were traditionally made of porcelain, silver, pewter, glass, and ceramic and came in all shapes and sizes. A local inn might have a lidded ceramic vessel decorated with colorful imagery and glazes, while the household of a wealthy merchant or member of the gentry might have a silver or crystal punch bowl of significantly larger size with far more ornamentation. Not surprisingly, as with all fads and crazes, the punch bowl became a status symbol, and the cost and design of the bowl were markers of the owner's fortunes.

The different ways in which people drank from punch bowls also dictated the vessels' design. During the 1600s it would be considered completely normal to drink directly from the bowl, with revelers passing it around the table to allow everyone to drink his fill. Consequently, the bowls were simple, round, and fitted with a lip that made it possible for even the most intoxicated patrons to drink from it without drooling onto their shirtfronts. Taverns would charge tables for these punch bowls depending on the size of the bowl and the amount of liquor it held. A "double" held two quarts of punch, while a "thribble" held three quarts.

> **⌐ Punch bowls were traditionally made of porcelain, silver, pewter, glass, and ceramic and came in all shapes and sizes**

One can only imagine what went on at these taverns, considering that at one recorded event, one group of eighty people drank eighty-two bowls of punch and eighteen bottles of wine. In those days, punch was made primarily of alcohol and very few "soft" ingredients, so even if those bowls were only doubles it was a miracle that any of the participants lived to tell the tale.

"View of a Skittle Ground at Hampstead" (1813), artist unknown. *Then, as now, bowling (or "skittles") involved the consumption of lots of alcohol, as evidenced by the bowl of punch being enjoyed by these jolly athletes.*

As the punch bowl found its way into genteel society, of course, punch drinkers began to sip from glasses. In the final two decades of the seventeenth century, a new style of bowl came into fashion, a "monteith," a fluted silver vessel named after a Scottish dandy known as "Monsieur Monteigh." Like the fashionable gentleman's coattails, which he wore with a jaunty notch between them, the rim of the monteith was scalloped, allowing glasses to be hung by their feet and to cool in ice placed inside the bowl. Over time, the addition of a removable corona, or rim, fitted with a strainer converted these wineglass-coolers into proper punch bowls. The strainer made it possible to lift various flavoring agents from the punch when it was ready to drink. The monteith, which eventually was made of many materials, from ceramic to glass, enjoyed immense popularity well into the Victorian era.

Beyond the monteith and its humbler cousins—the posset pot, caudle cup, wassail bowl, and others—punch bowls kept their basic basin shape throughout the centuries. Some were lidded, others were open, and others still had little hooks and clamps attached to their sides from which punch-drinking accoutrements could hang. Glasses, ladles, cups, and straws were the usual accessories to the punch bowl and would frequently be attached to it, creating an indispensable set for the generous host. An engraving from the mid-1800s shows a group of celebrants at a ball sipping punch directly from the bowl using what appears to be metal straws. The artist deftly captured an unexpected bit of casual slurping, proving that no matter how tight one's corset was laced, the temptation to dive face first into the punch bowl was, and remains, a strong one.

～ Punch bowls usually found their way into households as gifts, as they were considered the *ne plus ultra* of wedding presents

Of perhaps even more interest than the multitude of lavish and gorgeous punch bowls that have been manufactured over the years are the various and unexpected ways in which those bowls have been used. The "one item, one purpose" attitude we have toward our kitchen and dining room paraphernalia today didn't apply in bygone centuries. Indeed, the punch bowl was seen as a multipurpose vessel, the imagination of its owner being the only limit to its uses.

Punch bowls usually found their way into households as gifts, as they were considered the *ne plus ultra* of wedding presents. Sometimes, the bowl was given by an employer to his employee. This was particularly the custom in the shipping or maritime trade; it would be entirely proper, for instance, for the owner of a ship to present his captain with a punch bowl as a sign of gratitude for a job well done.

Once a family had the punch bowl in its place of honor on the sideboard, the bowl was put to work. When the vessel wasn't filled to the brim with an aromatic elixir, it might be doing double duty as a fruit bowl, an ice bucket,

DOULTON BURSLEM FOOTED PUNCH BOWL (c. 1880)
English ceramic, blue and white transfer

or even a baptismal font. In fact, employing the punch bowl for baptisms was one of its most common alternative uses and was an important part of what gave the punch bowl such a prized position in the household. By virtue of its center-stage performance in one of the family's most important and sacred events, the punch bowl itself was imbued with immense significance, which made serving punch from it to special guests an even more festive and heartfelt occasion (albeit, from a remove of several centuries, a little gross).

If having a baby dipped into your punch bowl strikes you as a little unsanitary, some of the practices at lavish fetes thrown by royalty and the aristocracy in punch's heyday were even more off-putting. For truly enormous gatherings, the traditional bowl was dispensed with altogether. In its place, a much larger vessel would do the honors. And what could be more madcap or festive than a mossy, outdoor fountain converted into a massive punch bowl, as one Admiral Edward Russell did in the Spanish port city of Alicante in October 1694? Out came the ornamental fish and flora and in went cask after cask of spirits, lime juice, sweeteners, and spices, as well as a miniature navy of boys who took turns sailing around the fountain in a skiff, ladling punch into cups for the attendees.

> **Employing the punch bowl for baptisms was one of its most common alternative uses and was an important part of what gave the punch bowl such a prized position in the household**

Another once-infamous punch bowl made in the late eighteenth century was owned by Englishman George Dickinson, a profiteer of the African slave trade. It was nearly two feet in diameter, made of Liverpool Delft, and painted with landscapes and ocean-crossing ships. It bears the inscription, "Success to the Africa Trade, George Dickinson," which caused a later ceramics expert to remark that it was a "wonder the punch didn't poison the drinkers." A bigger Delft bowl

"Anacreontick's in Full Song" (1801), by James Gilroy. *The Royal Anacreontic Society was an exclusive club for gentlemen with a fondness for song and drink. One of its most famous members was English musicologist and composer (and hard drinker) J. Stafford Smith, one of whose compositions later became the basis for "The Star-Spangled Banner."*

graced the buffet at the first Continental Congress. And an even more oceanic bowl played a part in the life of Thomas Jefferson. Jefferson's father apparently laid claim to the four hundred acres on which his famous son was born by trading his "biggest punch-bowl full of arrack punch" for the parcel. Not only did these vessels sport the symbols of, and bear witness to, historic events, they also occasionally served as the coin of the realm.

ROYAL FURNIVALS ENGLAND RUSTIC PATTERN FOOTED PUNCH BOWL (c. 1890)
Frolicking Bacchus transfer decoration, scalloped rim with luster finish

If this brief, colorful history of the punch bowl and the potions it has housed doesn't inspire admiration (or thirst), perhaps a sampling of poetry and doggerel that have graced them will. As you prepare to whip up a bowl of taste-tempting punch or its cousins—posset, wassail, caudle, aqua mirabilis, or usquebarb, for instance—think of these lines, lovingly penned in 1731 by punch-drunk imbibers of yore in praise of the fine Luxillion tin used to make the bowl's glaze:

> *John Udy of Luxillion*
> *His tin was so fine*
> *It glidered this punch-bowl*
> *And made it to shine*
>
> *Pray fill it with punch,*
> *Let the tinners fill round,*
> *They never will budge*
> *Till the bottom they sound*

And from a slightly more elevated enthusiast, Oliver Wendell Holmes, the opening lines of his "On Lending a Punch Bowl":

> *This ancient silver bowl of mine it tells of good old times*
> *Of joyous days, and jolly nights, and merry Christmas chimes;*
> *They were a free and jovial race, but honest, brave, and true,*
> *That dipped their ladle in the punch when this old bowl was new.*

So as you toast punch's recent resurgence with some of the concoctions featured in this book, drink deep and don't hold back. Get out your best quill or fountain pen and let the bacchanalian spirit move you as you sip your favorite elixir. Perhaps you too will be remembered for your love of all things punch long after your last bowl has been emptied.

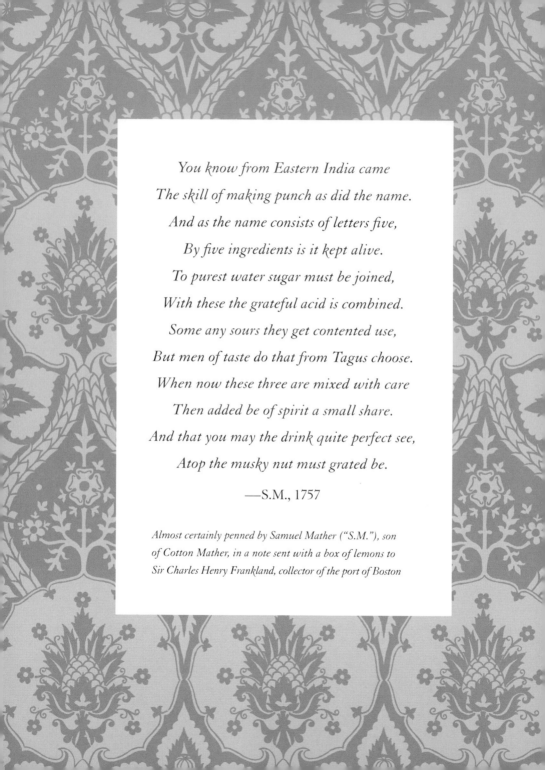

You know from Eastern India came
The skill of making punch as did the name.
And as the name consists of letters five,
By five ingredients is it kept alive.
To purest water sugar must be joined,
With these the grateful acid is combined.
Some any sours they get contented use,
But men of taste do that from Tagus choose.
When now these three are mixed with care
Then added be of spirit a small share.
And that you may the drink quite perfect see,
Atop the musky nut must grated be.

—S.M., 1757

Almost certainly penned by Samuel Mather ("S.M."), son
of Cotton Mather, in a note sent with a box of lemons to
Sir Charles Henry Frankland, collector of the port of Boston

THE ART OF SERVICE

THE ABILITY TO MAKE A GREAT PUNCH was once a point of pride and an essential skill for anyone entertaining friends and guests. Punch makers of repute caution that one must exercise great attention when crafting punch, as seen in the testimony of

"Bully" Dawson (a notorious seventeenth-century Londoner and punch maker, nicknamed for his skirmishes) in the 1869 book *Cups and Their Customs,* by George Edwin Roberts and Henry Porter:

> *The man who sees, does, or thinks of anything else while he is making Punch may as well look for the Northwest Passage on Mutton Hill. A man can never make good punch unless he is satisfied, nay positive, that no man breathing can make better. I can and do make good Punch, because I do nothing else, and this is my way of doing it . . . I retire to a solitary corner with my ingredients ready sorted; they are as follows, and I mix them in the order they are here written. Sugar, twelve tolerable lumps; hot water, one pint; lemons, two, the juice and peel; old Jamaica rum, two gills; brandy, one gill; porter or stout, half a gill; arrack, a slight dash. I allow myself five minutes to make a bowl in the foregoing proportions, carefully stirring the mixture as I furnish the ingredients until it actually foams; and then Kangaroos! How beautiful it is!*

"Kangaroos," indeed! Before you begin making punch, consider these essential tips and techniques.

Use High-Quality Liquors

"High quality" does not necessarily mean the most expensive or widely known liquor brands. For instance, if a punch recipe calls for brandy, it does not follow that an expensive aged Cognac (also a brandy) will be better than something that costs a third of the price. You can make great punches and still be budget friendly (though you should never use cheap rotgut or grain alcohol, either).

Page 31: WMF HAND-BLOWN CRYSTAL GLOBULAR-SHAPED PUNCH BOWL (C. 1920S), *mounted on silver plate stand with handles and matching top, Germany*

Plymouth Gin	*Rémy Martin V.S.O.P. Cognac*
Chartreuse	*Grand Solage Boulard Calvados*
Noilly Prat Dry Vermouth	*St. Germain Elderflower Liqueur*
Appleton Jamaica Rum	*van Oosten Batavia-Arrack*

Syrups

All syrups can be made by hand, but some are far simpler to purchase—orgeat, for instance, which is made from almonds, sugar, and rose- or orange-flower water.

As its name suggests, **simple syrup** is easy to make: Take one part sugar, one part water, and heat them to combine. It is in the application of heat where things become a touch more complicated. Boiling the sugar alters the character of the syrup, making it sweeter and less viscous, which is why it is recommended to boil the water first, remove the water from heat, and then pour in the sugar. Whisk the mixture until the granules have dissolved, and cool.

| *The Ginger People* | *Flavorganics* | *Stirrings* | *Trader Tiki's* |
| *Ginger Syrup* | *Raspberry Syrup* | *Blood Orange Bitters* | *Orgeat Syrup* |

Simple syrup will generally last up to a month in a tightly sealed glass jar in the refrigerator, but is still usable as long as it has not developed any mold or discoloration. (Adding a liquor capful of vodka before storage will help the syrup to keep longer.)

Fruit syrups require a little extra work, but are superior to most pre-bottled varieties. They call for fruit juice or purée, so first select ripe fruits, and either purée or juice them. For instance, for **passion fruit syrup**: Scoop the fruit from the shell, purée it, and then, using cheesecloth or a fine sieve, strain the purée until the juice is extracted from the pulp. Next, combine the purée or juice with small amounts of simple syrup

---

HELLO, SUGAR

As sweetness is a basic element in the making of punch, sugar appears in almost all punch recipes in one form or another. In this book, you will find recipes that call for demerara sugar, white sugar, light brown sugar, dark brown sugar, muscovado sugar, and powdered sugar. You may substitute confectioner's sugar for powdered sugar, but you'll be adding cornstarch, an ingredient in confectioner's sugar to prevent clumping, to your punch. Instead, create your own powdered sugar by pouring white sugar into the bowl of your food processor and grinding away until the sugar is the texture of superfine powder.

FALERNUM SYRUP

Falernum syrup is available commercially, but it is worth making yourself. This recipe comes from Phoebe Esmon, the head bartender at Chick's Café and Wine Bar in Philadelphia.

To make your falernum syrup you'll need fifty cloves, ten whole allspice, one-third cup chopped dried cinnamon bark, one whole nutmeg, the zest of nine limes, a one-inch piece of fresh ginger that has been chopped, fifteen unblanched, chopped almonds, one cup Wray & Nephew Rum, and one cup of simple syrup made with muscovado sugar.

1. First break up the cloves, allspice, and cinnamon a bit with a mortar and pestle. Don't grind them, just leave them cracked. The nutmeg should be grated a bit into the mix, with the rest dropped in whole. Put the spices in a jar and add the lime zest, ginger, almonds, and rum. Seal the jar by placing plastic film over the mouth before screwing on the lid. Let this mixture rest, unrefrigerated, for seventy-two hours, shaking it once a day.

2. Next, strain the mixture through a mesh sieve lined with unbleached cheesecloth. Discard the solids. Add the simple syrup and mix thoroughly. You now have authentic falernum syrup for all your various punch needs! Store in the refrigerator.

until the mixture achieves the desired sweetness. For **citrus syrups**, start with a one-to-one ratio of simple syrup to juice. For **fresh berry syrups**, add a very small amount of simple syrup initially and continue tasting the mixture to get it just right as you add more syrup.

There is another technique you can use for rich, delicate fruits such as strawberries or raspberries. Simply pour sugar on top of the fruit in a bowl until the fruit is coated. Cover the bowl and refrigerate the mixture. Leave the fruit to macerate overnight and the syrup will make itself. The fruit will be pulpy and broken down, and the syrup will be at the bottom of the bowl. Press the contents of the bowl through cheesecloth or a fine sieve and adjust, if necessary, with the addition of more simple syrup.

Fresh Is Best

Make sure that your fruit is fresh, wax-free (often fruit is covered in wax at supermarkets and needs to be carefully cleaned before use), and, when possible, in season. When using juices, opt for natural versus pre-sweetened and/or pasteurized juices, which will yield concoctions that are sugary, flat, and lacking in the aromatic qualities that make a good punch so appealing. The same goes for herbs and vegetables: the fresher, the better. Frequenting your local farmers' market or becoming an educated produce shopper will improve your punches. Recipes that call for canned fruit do so on purpose, but canned produce should not be used as a substitute for fresh.

When Recipes Hand You Lemons . . .

Citrus fruit can be temperamental, sometimes yielding abundant juice and at other times barely a few drops. Here are some tips for getting the most out of your citrus:

~ Squeeze citrus only when it's warm, i.e., not taken directly from your refrigerator. If need be, you can soak the citrus in hot water for a few minutes to bring it to room temperature, or microwave it for ten seconds.

~ An old kitchen trick is to roll the fruit before squeezing. Simply place the fruit between the palm of your hand and the countertop and roll back and forth several times while applying gentle downward pressure.

~ Invest in an electric citrus squeezer for lemons and limes, and a reamer for larger citrus fruits like large oranges or grapefruit. Squeezing citrus can be an arduous task—especially when you have twenty lemons to juice—making these tools well worth the storage space.

~ It's fine to peel citrus directly out of the refrigerator. But whenever cutting the peels away from the fruit, use only the zest and not the pith, which has a bitter taste. A quality zester is an excellent tool to have around, though a sharp paring knife or vegetable peeler will do the trick.

Fruit Garnishes and Decorative Touches

There are endless ways to dress up a punch bowl, punch glasses, or even the table you've set up for your punch service. Here are a few ideas to get you started, but let your own sense of style and whimsy be your guide. The only limit is your own imagination.

~ When garnishing with fruit, it's helpful to know how many slices a particular fruit will yield. Depending on how handy you are with a knife, the results may vary, but generally an apple will yield sixteen slices. A pear will yield about twelve to sixteen slices depending on the size, and oranges will yield about ten or twelve slices.

~ If preparing apples or pears as garnishes ahead of party time, keep your slices in a bowl filled with water and the juice of one lemon, which will prevent the fruit from browning.

~ Strawberries are a terrific garnish. Their bright red color and shape are always inviting, and they are firm enough to balance on the edge of a glass once a slit has been cut in the berry.

~ To float strawberries in a punch, try slicing them lengthwise but leaving the top with the leaves intact. Fan the slices out and float the little fans in the punch.

~ Other berries that work well in punch are blackberries, blueberries, and firm red or yellow raspberries. They won't disintegrate and will add lovely color and texture.

~ Use a small ice cream scoop or melon baller to form spheres of fruit. Float them in the punch bowl or add the balls to a glass before pouring the punch.

~ Slice firm fruit into one-quarter-inch thick pieces, and then use cookie cutters in a variety of shapes to create decorations to float in the punch.

~ Place sliced fruit on a skewer or toothpick, and then set it across the rim of a punch cup.

~ Cut thin twists of the rinds of any citrus fruit, tie them in a knot, and float them in your punch glasses.

~ Forgo punch cups entirely and use the carefully scraped and cleaned hollowed out rinds of any citrus fruit to hold your punch.

~ Fresh cherries are a delicacy, but they require a little surgery before serving. You can easily transform any pitted cherry into a charming flower by slicing one end into six wedges (leave the bottom third of the cherry intact) and then gently pushing down on the wedges. The result is a flower with six petals made of cherry. Float them in your punch cup or in your punch bowl.

~ If you are serving a punch loaded with fall fruits, such as apples, pears, or citrus, try dressing up your table with those same fruits fashioned as candleholders. Simply cut the fruit so it has a flat bottom and, with a paring knife, core a hole at the top that will snugly fit the diameter of your candle or votive.

The Dilution Solution

One of the core issues with making a punch is reaching the proper dilution and temperature (both of which are intimately connected) for service. Many recipes are pre-diluted—for instance, those that call for the addition of water or tea, or those that will be served warm—and any additional dilution will lead to watery or weak punches. Hardly worthy of its origins as a sailor's drink! Therefore, using a large block of ice in cold punches is preferable to chipped ice or cubes—the larger the block you use, the better, because larger blocks melt more slowly.

One way to make block ice is by filling a medium loaf pan or bowl with water and freezing it solid—for larger punch bowls, a Bundt pan works well.

Always use filtered or bottled water, if possible. If you do use water from the tap, boil it first to remove as many impurities and off-flavors as possible. Clean water means clean ice. Finally, the block can be filled with slices of mixed fruit and/or edible flowers before freezing to create a decorative and functional block of ice.

When serving warm punch, do not boil any ingredient except for water, lest the aromatic qualities be diminished and the alcohol evaporate. Serve warm punches immediately after warming them.

Edible Flower Garnishes and Decorative Touches

Flowers add bursts of color and the polished elegance that every entertainer strives for.

The guiding principle of garnishing punch with flowers is simple: Use whole flowers when you are floating them in your punch bowl, for maximum impact; when garnishing a drink, candied flowers, flower petals, and tiny flower buds are the way to go. It's never fun to sip a glass of punch while an entire peony blossom careens toward your nose!

The Edibles

Be sure to select nontoxic floral varieties—nothing's worse than a convivial gathering punctuated by a fevered rush to the emergency room. Likewise, make sure to get flowers that haven't been sprayed with pesticides or other harmful chemicals. Listed below are edible flowers you can use freely as a garnish in any punch, as well as ideas for displaying the blooms to their best advantage.

~ borage flowers	~ honeysuckle	~ passionflowers
~ carnations	~ lavender	~ peony petals
~ daylilies	~ lilacs	~ primroses
~ freesia	~ marigolds	~ roses or rose petals
~ gardenias	~ nasturtiums	~ snapdragons
~ gladiolus	~ orange blossoms	~ sunflowers
~ hibiscus	~ pansies	~ violets

1. Remove the stamen and pistil from the flowers.
2. Clean the flowers by shaking them gently, and then use a fine, soft spray of water to cleanse the petals.
3. Set the flowers on kitchen towels to air dry.

Neglect this preparation and your guests will find bits of pollen and flower innards floating in their punch, and the flowers will wilt more quickly.

Carnation   Sunflower   Tulip

Snapdragon   Marigold   Daylilies

Just Candy

Candied flowers frequently show up on top of cakes and other baked treats, but can just as easily serve as a garnish in any punch. Don't be intimidated; candying flowers is very easy. You'll need a small, soft paintbrush, a flat surface, parchment paper or aluminum foil, granulated sugar, and water. After your blooms are cleaned and dried, apply a mixture of equal parts water and sugar to the flowers with the paintbrush. Let them dry on the parchment or foil, and reapply the sugar mixture until the flowers look like they are glittering. They will harden into a fixed shape as they dry. Float your candied flowers in punch glasses for a dash of color *and* sweetness. If you're pressed for time, the good news is that candied violets are readily available in most specialty stores.

Measure for Measure

Always use measuring cups and spoons when mixing your punch. Making punches is more akin to baking than savory cooking. Since the flavor of the punch develops over time, it is crucial to remember that adjustments to the amounts of each ingredient that is added will have a magnified effect once the flavors have settled.

Allspice   *Cinnamon*   *Cloves*   *Mint*

Nutmeg   *Cardamom Pods*   *Mace*   *Green Tea*

BOUQUET GARNI

Herbs can easily be added to punches by creating a bouquet garni. The literal definition is a "garnished bouquet," and most cooks know it as a combination of thyme, parsley, and bay leaf used to flavor soups. But a bouquet garni can be made with any combination of herbs, and it makes infusing punch with herbal flavors extremely simple since it's a cinch to pull it out of the punch before serving.

   To create a bouquet garni, bundle the herbs you are using together with a piece of undyed kitchen twine or string, making sure that everything is secured in the package so that nothing will float free in the punch. Do not cover the herbs in anything else—like cheesecloth—as this will inhibit the ability of the oils of the herbs to infuse the liquid. When the punch is ready, you can easily remove the bouquet garni from the liquid with a slotted spoon, and you're ready to serve.

The Under and Over of Steeping Tea

When recipes call for tea, it's imperative to steep the tea properly. In general, follow the directions on the box of tea, keeping in mind what the recipe is calling for (sometimes you will be instructed to over- or under-steep a tea). Here are some guidelines for steeping tea, either bagged or loose.

TEA TIME AND TEMPS
Black tea: 3 to 5 minutes; water temperature: 203°F*
Green tea: 1 to 2 minutes; water temperature: 150 to 160°F
Oolong (partially fermented black tea): 1 to 9 minutes; water temperature: 203°F
White tea: 4 to 15 minutes; water temperature: 185°F
Herbal tea: 5 to 10 minutes; water temperature: 203°F
*The boiling point of water is 212°F, but water for tea should be cooler

Feeling loose? Intense and delicious, loose teas are a great alternative to the humdrum bagged variety. Measure a scant teaspoon per cup of tea you are preparing. Mesh tea balls or paper tea filters, both available at tea shops and some supermarkets, are perfect when you do not want to bother with straining tea leaves. Fill the ball or filter (remember to seal the filter bag), add the hot water, and steep according to your recipe or the type of tea you are using. Loose teas can also be added directly to hot water. Steep as directed, then strain out the leaves.

If the recipe lists a strong tea, use a strongly flavored black tea like Assam (unless it specifies that you use a strongly flavored green tea). In some cases, cold steeping may be the best way to extract delicate flavors with minimal sharp, bitter, or tannic flavors. Cold steeping takes longer, requiring between six to twelve hours. Simply set the tea bags in room-temperature water, cover, and taste after six hours to see if the tea has infused properly. If the tea isn't strong enough, continue steeping, tasting every hour until you achieve the desired strength. Either way, when brewing tea, use freshly filtered or spring water.

Let the Flavors Get Acquainted

To ensure the proper integration of flavors in your punch, it is important to let most mixtures sit at room temperature for an hour or two and then in the refrigerator for an additional two hours. Some types of punch need to be warmed up, of course, but whichever is the case, the ingredients need time to settle and combine.

How Much to Make

When planning how much punch to make for your gathering, consider who your guests are and the function of your party. Is it a gathering of friends or business colleagues? Do the guests know each other or is this their first time meeting? (The answers will generally affect the rate of consumption, and the amount you will need to make; for instance, strangers often don't want to appear to be heavy drinkers, even if they really are.)

Harrach Amethyst Overlay Cut to Clear Punch Bowl (c. 1940s), *featuring gold overlay, Germany*

If you know your guests personally, ask yourself the following questions: are they light, moderate, or heavy drinkers? If they are a mix of all three, you'll have to split the difference.

Light drinkers are likely to "graze," or sip approximately one punch cup (4 to 5 ounces) per person/per hour and will usually stop after one.

Moderate drinkers generally "sip and talk," drinking one and a half punch cups (6 to 8 ounces) per person/per hour.

Heavy drinkers will "put back a few" drinks at two punch cups (8 to 10 ounces) per person/per hour. Although there is a plateau at which, after two hours of heavy drinking, it is likely that your guests' drinking will subside. At that point there is a diminishing rate at which heavy drinkers become moderate, the moderate become light, and the light move to water.

Therefore, with ten guests of mixed enthusiasm for drinking, you may assume the median (7 ounces) per person/per hour. If it's a two-hour party, then a little more than a gallon (which is 128 ounces) will be required. As others have rightly said, quality is more important than quantity, so whatever quantity you set on the table, make sure it's delicious.

Despite the many guidelines for making punch and the effort that goes into the process, a properly crafted bowl of punch is the ultimate lubricant for any gathering. Your guests will recognize the care and effort you put into their enjoyment, and their spirits will certainly rise, but more importantly, they will remember how much fun you had with them at your party. One of the greatest virtues of a bowl of punch—which provides the very best sort of self-service—is that it enables the host to participate more fully, and to relax more, at the party.

NOTE: Throughout this book, one serving has been calculated as approximately one 4- to 6-ounce cup of punch.

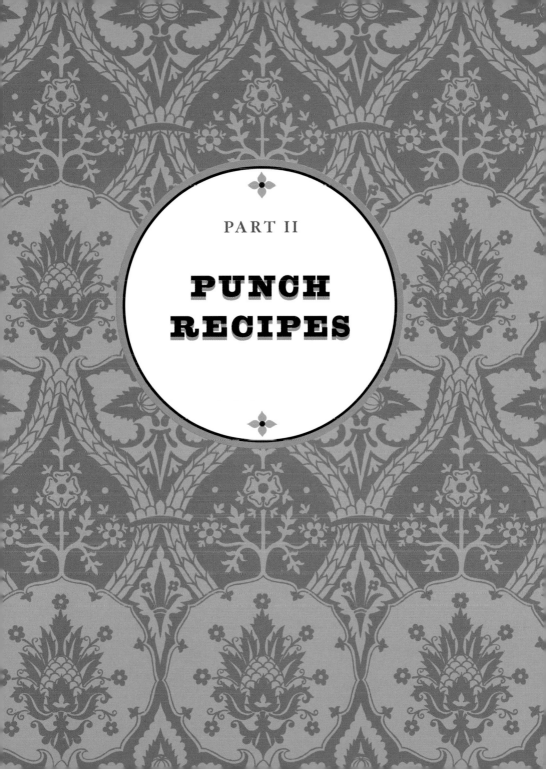

PART II

PUNCH RECIPES

1.

RUM PUNCHES

"I pity them greatly, but I must be mum,
for how could we do without sugar and rum?"

—WILLIAM COWPER, English poet, 1731–1800

PUNCH À LA ROMAINE

From Jerry Thomas' Bartenders Guide: How to Mix Drinks, *1862*

━━━━━━━━━━━━━━━━━━━ ◎ ━━━━━━━━━━━━━━━━━━━

WITH A LIGHT AND AIRY TEXTURE, this punch can easily replace a sorbet as the palate cleanser in a sumptuous feast. In fact, it did, famously, as the sixth course served on the RMS *Titanic* in the first-class drinking room before the ship's epic demise. Not to disparage the *Titanic*'s crew, but it would be best to avoid operating heavy machinery after drinking.

~ *10 to 15 servings*

INGREDIENTS

1 ½ CUPS LEMON JUICE
(ABOUT 10 LEMONS)
½ CUP ORANGE JUICE, FRESHLY SQUEEZED
(ABOUT 2 ORANGES)
2 CUPS POWDERED SUGAR (SEE PAGE 34)
RIND OF ONE ORANGE, THINLY SLICED
10 EGG WHITES
1 750-ML BOTTLE DARK RUM
1 750 ML BOTTLE DRY WHITE WINE

1. Combine the citrus juice in a large mixing bowl. Add the sugar, and stir until dissolved. Add the orange rind. Stir, then let the juice mixture rest for at least 1 hour.

2. Strain the juice mixture through a fine sieve into a large punch bowl.

3. In a separate mixing bowl, beat the egg whites until frothy but not stiff. Slowly stir the egg whites into the juice mixture. Place the punch bowl in the refrigerator, and chill for at least 1 hour.

4. Immediately before serving, briskly stir in the rum and the wine.

A NOTE ABOUT USING EGGS: Using raw eggs in any recipe carries with it the remote possibility of causing illness. If you decide to make a punch recipe that calls for raw eggs or raw egg whites, make sure to find the freshest eggs possible (check the date on the carton if you're not using farm-fresh eggs), and wash and rinse the outside of the eggs carefully before cracking them open. Always proceed with caution and let your guests (especially those who are elderly or pregnant) know you have used raw eggs in the preparation of the punch.

Page 49: FURNIVALS ENGLAND FOOTED PUNCH BOWL (c. 1890), *Greek transfer decoration, hand-colored polychrome enamel decoration with gold trim*

RUM PUNCH

From Modern American Drinks, *1895*

⟨≋⟩

YOUR CHOICE OF RUM will make or break this punch. Opt for strong sugar-based liquor like arrack, or aged rums from Jamaica and Martinique. Remember, this is a sailor's punch and, as such, was intended to pack a sufficient wallop to weather choppy seas. If you prefer a more flavorful and brisk punch, substitute an equal amount of brewed tea for the seltzer water (in addition to the tea already called for).

⟿ *20 to 30 servings*

INGREDIENTS

2 CUPS BREWED BLACK TEA

½ CUP DEMERARA SUGAR, PLUS MORE
   TO TASTE

4 CUPS BRANDY

2 CUPS LIGHT OR DARK RUM

½ CUP PEACH BRANDY

1 CUP LEMON JUICE (ABOUT 6 LEMONS)

1 TO 1½ QUARTS SELTZER WATER

OPTIONAL

½ CUP CURAÇAO OR OTHER ORANGE
   LIQUEUR

½ TO 1 CUP STRAWBERRIES, HULLED
   AND SLICED

½ TO 1 CUP CHERRIES, PITTED AND SLICED

½ TO 1 CUP PINEAPPLE, SLICED

1. Put the tea and sugar into a large punch bowl and stir until the sugar is dissolved. Add the brandy, rum, and peach brandy, and stir well. Add the lemon juice to the punch and stir. Put the punch bowl in the refrigerator, and chill for at least 2 hours.

2. When ready to serve, add the carbonated water slowly, and gently stir the punch. Taste as you go, adding less carbonated water if you want a stronger punch. If you'd like a fruitier punch, you can add the Curaçao and any combination of the sliced fruits.

TAHITIAN RUM PUNCH

Adapted from a recipe by Ernest Gantt, 1939

ORIGINALLY CREATED by Ernest Gantt (who later changed his name to Donn Beach), the founder of legendary bar Don's Beachcomber Café and widely regarded as the godfather of Tiki culture. The fruit and rums blend seamlessly, suggesting a relaxing trip to a faraway tropical destination. As Beach was purported to have said, "If you can't get to paradise, I'll bring it to you."

30 to 45 servings

INGREDIENTS:

- 4 CUPS ORANGE JUICE, FRESHLY SQUEEZED (ABOUT 16 ORANGES), RINDS RESERVED
- 1½ CUPS LEMON JUICE (ABOUT 12 LEMONS), RINDS RESERVED
- ¾ CUP GRAPEFRUIT JUICE, FRESHLY SQUEEZED (ABOUT 1 GRAPEFRUIT), RIND RESERVED
- 3½ BANANAS, SLICED
- 1 CUP DARK BROWN SUGAR
- 2 SPRIG FRESH MINT
- 2½ 750-ML BOTTLES DRY WHITE WINE
- 1½ 1-L BOTTLES LIGHT RUM
- 1 CUP DARK JAMAICAN RUM

1. Strain the orange, lemon, and grapefruit juices into a very large mixing bowl or container, and add the rinds of all the fruit. Add the banana and sugars to the mixture. Add the mint and white wine, and stir well. Refrigerate the punch overnight.

2. At least 4 hours before serving, add the rums to the chilled punch. Strain the punch into a large punch bowl filled with ice cubes, and serve.

JAMAICAN PUNCH

~ *Circa 1655* ~

ORIGINALLY, THE FINAL INGREDIENT in this punch was pimento, a bit confusing since most people assume that it refers to the tiny red peppers stuffed into cocktail olives. Pimento is, in fact, the Jamaican term for allspice, which originated from the Spanish word "pimienta," or peppercorns. The tiny berries are extremely flavorful and are also used in Jamaican jerk recipes.

12 to 18 servings

INGREDIENTS

1 CUP FRESH LIME JUICE
(ABOUT 8 LIMES)

2 CUPS SIMPLE SYRUP OR STRAWBERRY
SYRUP (SEE PAGES 33–35)

3 CUPS LIGHT RUM

4 CUPS WATER

GROUND ALLSPICE

1. In a punch bowl or a large pitcher, combine the lime juice and simple syrup until well blended. Slowly add the rum, stirring constantly.

2. Add the water 1 cup at a time, tasting as you go. Stop at 3 cups of water if you prefer a stronger punch. Add allspice to taste.

3. Serve in punch cups or lowball glasses filled with ice.

HOT RUM PUNCH

From Edward Hamilton, creator of the Ministry of Rum

—— ⚬➤⚬ ——

"DO SOMETHING YOU LOVE and you'll never work a day in your life." That's easy to say for Edward Hamilton. He's spent years sailing around the Caribbean learning about, and drinking, rum. Now, in addition to his efforts importing and teaching others about his favorite spirit, he oversees the Ministry of Rum, which he modestly calls "the most credible source of information about sugar cane spirits on the Internet."

Citrus and pineapple make this a tart, tropical twist on the classic winter treat: hot rum and cider.

20 to 30 servings

INGREDIENTS

1 TABLESPOON BUTTER
1 PINEAPPLE, PEELED AND CUT INTO LARGE CHUNKS
1 ORANGE, CUT IN EIGHTHS
½ LEMON, QUARTERED
4 TO 6 CINNAMON STICKS
24 WHOLE CLOVES
1 QUART ORANGE JUICE
2 QUARTS APPLE CIDER
2⅛ CUPS DARK RUM
1 CUP LIGHT RUM
20 TO 30 APPLE SLICES (ABOUT 2 APPLES)

1. Melt the butter in a large pot. If necessary, add more to cover the bottom of the pot. Add the pineapple chunks, and sauté until lightly browned. Add the orange, lemon, cinnamon sticks, and cloves. Add the orange juice and apple cider. Bring to a boil and simmer for 10 to 15 minutes.

2. Allow to cool, then refrigerate overnight.

3. To serve, add both rums, and heat the mixture until hot but not boiling. Garnish cups with a slice of apple.

TRADEWINDS PUNCH

From Jon Harris, The Gibson, Washington, D.C.

꧁꧂

APTLY NAMED, this punch takes the drinker on a trip around the world, featuring exotic ingredients from Europe, Asia, and the Americas. The most unusual ingredient in this concoction is the saffron gin. If you'd like to try variations on this recipe do so by using different India Pale Ales (IPA) each time you make it. IPA is a style of beer originally brewed with extra alcohol and hops to preserve the treasured beverage during the long voyage to and from England and India.

꧁ *24 to 36 servings*

INGREDIENTS

2 ⅛ CUPS EL DORADO 151 RUM
1 CUP GABRIEL BOUDIER SAFFRON GIN
2 VANILLA BEANS, SPLIT
 GRATED ZEST OF HALF A GRAPEFRUIT
3 FRESH, RIPE GUAVAS, THINLY SLICED
1 TABLESPOON CHINESE FIVE SPICE POWDER
1 STALK LEMONGRASS, SLICED
1 CUP FRESH LIME JUICE (ABOUT 8 LIMES)
2 ⅛ CUPS SIMPLE SYRUP (SEE PAGE 33)
4 ¼ CUPS WATER
7 12-OUNCE BOTTLES INDIA PALE ALE (BELL'S TWO HEARTED ALE RECOMMENDED)

1. Mix the first 7 ingredients in a container. Cover tightly, and let the mixture sit overnight. The next day, strain the liquid through cheesecloth. Add the juice, the syrup, and the water. Reserve.

2. To assemble the punch, add the IPA to the reserved spiced rum/gin mixture. Add ice. Garnish the punch with seasonal fruits, and serve.

FURNIVALS ENGLAND FOOTED PUNCH BOWL ~ CIRCA 1890

Greek transfer decoration, hand-colored polychrome enamel decoration with gold trim

AUTUMNAL PUNCH

Adapted from a recipe by H. Joseph Ehrmann, Elixir, San Francisco, California

SPICE IS ONE OF THE ESSENTIAL INGREDIENTS in a classic punch, and incorporating St. Elizabeth Allspice Dram into a punch is a great way to showcase that fact. A re-creation of the Jamaican Pimento Dram called for in many classic cocktails, this sweet and pungent liqueur can be overpowering on its own. It does, however, add a complex and distinctive note when used in small amounts and balanced by other strong flavors.

15 to 20 servings

INGREDIENTS

1 750-ML BOTTLE RHUM CLÉMENT V.S.O.P.

1 750-ML BOTTLE MARIE BRIZARD POIRE WILLIAMS

3¼ CUPS LEMON JUICE (ABOUT 18 LEMONS)

⅓ CUP ST. ELIZABETH'S ALLSPICE DRAM

¼ CUP ORGEAT SYRUP

RAISINS (PREFERABLY GOLDEN)

1. In a container, combine all ingredients and stir well.

2. Pour over an ice block into a punch bowl. Stir and serve. Garnish cups with raisins.

SCORPION PUNCH

Adapted from Trader Vic's Book of Food & Drink, *1946*

DONN BEACH may have been the founder of Tiki kitsch, but the better-known Tiki master is Victor Bergeron (aka Trader Vic). His Scorpion Punch is another delicious tropical adventure in a glass. In this version, the fruit juices have been diversified and the "sting" slightly increased.

~ *15 to 20 servings*

INGREDIENTS

  2 750-ML BOTTLES PUERTO RICAN RUM

¼ CUP GIN

¼ CUP BRANDY

  1 CUP LIME JUICE (ABOUT 8 LIMES)

  1 CUP ORANGE JUICE, FRESHLY SQUEEZED (ABOUT 4 ORANGES)

  1 CUP PINEAPPLE JUICE

  1 CUP ORGEAT SYRUP

  2 SPRIGS FRESH MINT

½ 750-ML BOTTLE DRY WHITE WINE

1. Mix together the rum, gin, brandy, lime, pineapple, and orange juices in a large bowl. Add the orgeat; slightly bruise the mint, and add it to the bowl. Add the white wine, stir well, and transfer the mixture to a large punch bowl. Put the bowl in the refrigerator, and chill for 2 hours.

2. When ready to serve, remove the bowl from the refrigerator, and add ice cubes.

PICKIN' PUNCH

From Derek Brown, The Passenger and the Columbia Room, Washington, D.C.

JUST AS A COLA made with cane sugar tastes different from one made with high fructose corn syrup, the type of sweetener you choose for a punch can make a big difference in the taste. Here, demerara sugar provides a complex, caramel note.

30 to 45 servings

INGREDIENTS

    PEELS OF 2 LEMONS

2 CUPS FINE DEMERARA SUGAR (SEE PAGE 34)

1 750-ML BOTTLE RHUM CLÉMENT V.S.O.P.

1 QUART APPLE CIDER

1 750-ML BOTTLE DARK RUM

1 750-ML BOTTLE LAIRD'S APPLEJACK

1⅔ CUPS BLENDED SCOTCH

½ GALLON SELTZER WATER

28 TO 40 APPLE SLICES (ABOUT 3 APPLES), FOR GARNISH

28 TO 40 CINNAMON STICKS, FOR GARNISH

1. In a large bowl, muddle the lemon peels with the sugar, and then add the apple cider. Stir in the rum, applejack, and scotch; refrigerate the mixture for two hours.

2. Pour it into a punch bowl over a large ice block. Add chilled seltzer water, and serve. Garnish cups with apple slices and cinnamon sticks.

FISH HOUSE PUNCH

~ Circa 1732 ~

A CONCOCTION SHROUDED IN SECRECY (and ongoing disagreement about its exact ingredients), this grand old recipe comes from the Schuylkill Fishing Company, one of America's oldest men's clubs, originally founded in 1732. Some prominent figures in American history, including George Washington, have enjoyed a glass or two of Fish House Punch at the famous club (which still exists today, though no longer in Schuylkill county). Sip this punch and open a window onto what might have made America's Founding Fathers feel so very revolutionary.

~ 15 to 20 servings

INGREDIENTS

4 CUPS LIME JUICE (ABOUT 32 LIMES)
2 CUPS LEMON JUICE (ABOUT 12 LEMONS)
1 CUP DARK BROWN SUGAR
1 CUP DARK RUM
2 CUPS LIGHT RUM
1 CUP BRANDY
1 BLOCK OF ICE

1. Pour the lemon and lime juices into a large punch bowl. Add the brown sugar, and gently stir until dissolved. Slowly add the dark and light rums and the brandy, stirring constantly. Slowly ease the block of ice into the punch bowl.

2. Put the punch bowl into the refrigerator, and chill for 3 hours. Stir the punch every few hours to help the flavors blend.

3. When ready to serve, remove the bowl from the refrigerator and, if need be, add more ice.

CARIBBEAN PUNCH

Adapted from Trader Vic's Book of Food & Drink, *1946*

THIS PUNCH INCLUDES A CURVEBALL INGREDIENT, falernum syrup, a delicious, sweet mixture traditionally made from clove, ginger, almond, lime, vanilla, and allspice.

⌐ *40 to 55 servings*

INGREDIENTS

    3 750-ML BOTTLES PUERTO RICAN RUM
    1 CUP JAMAICAN DARK RUM
    1 GALLON WATER
    2 CUPS LEMON JUICE (ABOUT 12 LEMONS)
    ½ CUP CURAÇAO OR OTHER ORANGE
        LIQUEUR
    1 20-OUNCE CAN SLICED PINEAPPLE
    1 PINT FRESH RASPBERRIES
    3 ORANGES, SLICED
        FALERNUM SYRUP (SEE PAGE 35)

1. Combine the rums, water, lemon juice, and Curaçao in a large bowl. Add the pineapple, raspberries, and orange slices, and stir. Add the falernum to taste, 1 tablespoon at a time, then pour the mixture into a large punch bowl.

2. Put a large block of ice in the bowl and transfer the bowl to the refrigerator. Chill the punch for 1 hour before serving.

RUBY PUNCH

From Cooling Cups and Dainty Drinks, *1869*

THIS PUNCH MAKES a perfect aperitif and is a delightful start to any evening. To achieve depth of flavor in this punch, use a good tawny port. If you are looking for a more budget-friendly substitution, ruby port will do the trick.

15 to 20 servings

INGREDIENTS

6 CUPS BREWED GREEN TEA (BREWED WEAK)

2 CUPS DEMERARA SUGAR

1 CUP LEMON JUICE, STRAINED (ABOUT 6 LEMONS)

2 CUPS ARRACK

2 CUPS TAWNY PORT

1. In a large punch bowl, combine the green tea and half of the sugar, stirring until the sugar is dissolved.

2. Add the lemon juice, and stir well. Add the arrack and port, and mix well. If you'd like a sweeter punch, add more sugar to taste.

3. Before serving, add several cups of ice cubes to the bowl.

CUTLER'S RUM PUNCH

From Cooling Cups and Dainty Drinks, *1869*

IN THE WONDERFULLY QUIRKY and educational recipe book *Cooling Cups and Dainty Drinks* the term "oleo-saccharum," the mixture of oil and sugar, comes up frequently. In the original recipe for this punch, the oleo-saccharum is created by muddling the lemon zest and sugar together so the lemon peel releases its fragrant oil into the sugar.

15 to 20 servings

INGREDIENTS

1 CUP DEMERARA SUGAR
   GRATED ZEST OF 2 LEMONS
½ CUP LEMON JUICE (ABOUT 3 LEMONS)
1 750-ML BOTTLE BRANDY
2 CUPS DARK RUM
1 CUP SHERRY
1 QUART BOILING WATER
   FRESHLY GRATED NUTMEG

1. In a large punch bowl, muddle the sugar and the grated lemon zest with a wooden spoon. Add the lemon juice, and stir well. Add the brandy, rum, and sherry; add the boiling water, and stir well. Grate the nutmeg into the punch to taste, but it's best with just a little.

2. Let the punch rest for 5 to 10 minutes, depending on whether you want to serve it hot or cold. If you want to enjoy this punch cold, add ice cubes to the punch bowl after 10 minutes.

TRINIDAD PUNCH

From Cooling Cups and Dainty Drinks, *1869*

TRINIDAD PUNCH is the chocolate milk of the punch world. It's rich and creamy and as satisfying as a dessert but still has a bracing kick. Trinidad Punch can be served cold but is also terrific warm, which makes it a great drink during the winter months. When making this punch, use chocolate made from at least 80% cacao to ensure the richest flavor possible.

8 to 12 servings

INGREDIENTS

- 2 CUPS DARK RUM
- 1 OUNCE GOOD-QUALITY DARK CHOCOLATE
- ½ VANILLA BEAN
- 4 CUPS THIN COCONUT MILK

1. Melt the chocolate in a double boiler.

2. Pour the rum into a large bowl. Split the vanilla bean in half and scrape the seeds into the rum before adding the bean. Add the chocolate, and stir until well blended.

3. Strain the punch into a punch bowl, and add the coconut milk. Mix well. Before serving, add as many ice cubes to the bowl as it will hold.

NOTE: This punch may also be served warm. Strain the punch except the rum into a large stockpot set over medium-high heat, and add the coconut milk. Stir constantly while the punch warms. Just before it begins to simmer, remove the pot from the heat, add the rum, and pour the punch into a punch bowl.

2.
BOURBON & WHISKEY PUNCHES

"Nothing is so musical as the sound of pouring bourbon for the first drink on a Sunday morning. Not Bach or Schubert or any of those masters."

—CARSON MCCULLERS,
from *Clock Without Hands*

SPREAD EAGLE PUNCH

From Jerry Thomas' Bartenders Guide: How to Mix Drinks, *1862*

THE SPREAD EAGLE PUNCH can be found in the famous *Bartenders Guide* written by "Professor" Jerry Thomas. The original recipe called for Monongahela whiskey, which is sadly no longer available. We have replaced it with Old Overholt, which does the trick. Monongahela whiskey, when it was still being produced, hailed from Monongahela, Pennsylvania, home of the Whiskey Rebellion of 1794 and a stop on the Underground Railroad.

12 to 18 servings

INGREDIENTS

½ CUP DEMERARA SUGAR
    GRATED ZEST OF 1 LEMON
1 CUP BOILING WATER
1 750-ML BOTTLE ISLAY SINGLE MALT
    SCOTCH WHISKEY
1 750-ML BOTTLE OLD OVERHOLT
    RYE WHISKEY

1. Muddle the sugar and lemon zest together in a mixing bowl with a wooden spoon until well incorporated. Add the boiling water, the Islay whiskey, and the Old Overholt. Place the mixture in the refrigerator, and chill for at least 2 hours.

2. Pour the punch into a punch bowl that has been filled with ice cubes.

Page 69: WEDGEWOOD "OLD VINE" PATTERN DIMINUTIVE PUNCH BOWL (c. 1930s), *transfer and hand-colored luster decoration*

OLD FAITHFUL

From Gina Chersevani, PS7's, Washington, D.C.

━━━━━━━━━━━━━━━━━━━━ ❧ ━━━━━━━━━━━━━━━━━━━━

WITH ITS RUSTICALLY NOSTALGIC PACKAGING, authentic 1830 recipe, and "Frontier Whiskey" moniker, Bulliet Bourbon seems like a natural place to start a good ol' punch. But add a bit of continental sophistication in the form of newly popular St. Germain, and this punch leaps forward into the twenty-first century. Together these two ingredients form the base of a punch that won't let you down whether you prefer to look where you're going or reflect on where you've been.

━━━

∽ *18 to 24 servings*

INGREDIENTS

  1 CUP POWDERED SUGAR (SEE PAGE 34)
  1 750-ML BOTTLE BULLIET BOURBON
1⅔ CUPS ST. GERMAIN ELDERFLOWER
    LIQUEUR
  4 CUPS PINK GRAPEFRUIT JUICE,
    FRESHLY SQUEEZED
    (ABOUT 4 GRAPEFRUIT)
 20 DASHES FEE BROTHERS GRAPEFRUIT
    BITTERS
  1 750-ML BOTTLE SPARKLING WATER
 30 MINT LEAVES
 20 STRIPS OF GRAPEFRUIT PEEL
    (ABOUT 2 GRAPEFRUIT)

1. In a large bowl, whisk together the powdered sugar, bourbon, and St. Germain until the sugar is completely dissolved. Add the pink grapefruit juice and the grapefruit bitters, and stir to combine.

2. Top the punch with the mint leaves and grapefruit peels, then stir gently and let the punch sit for about an hour. Immediately before serving add the sparkling water. Ladle into ice-filled glasses.

WHISKEY PUNCH À LA BARRETT

From Cooling Cups and Dainty Drinks, *1869*

〜🌀🌀〜

WILLIAM TERRINGTON writes in *Cooling Cups and Dainty Drinks* that, "guava or apple jelly make punches truly delicious." Well said, but make sure it is jelly and not apple butter. These jellies are suitable for use year-round to relieve you from having to hunt down quality seasonal fruit.

〜 *6 to 10 servings*

INGREDIENTS

   2 CUPS BOILING WATER
   2 TEASPOONS GUAVA OR APPLE JELLY
   2 CUPS WHISKEY

1. Pour the boiling water into a large mixing bowl, and whisk in the jelly until it is dissolved. Slowly add the whiskey, and stir well. Transfer the punch to the refrigerator, and chill for 3 hours.

2. To serve, pour the punch into a punch bowl that has been filled with ice cubes.

CANADIAN PUNCH

From Jerry Thomas' Bartenders Guide: How to Mix Drinks, *1862*

THOUGH NOT A FRUIT NATIVE TO CANADA, fresh pineapple is essential when mixing up a batch of Canadian Punch. Try to buy the pineapple the day you're planning to make the punch, and avoid any fruit that is mushy, leaking, or cracked. No matter what, don't use canned pineapple. The canned variety is heaven in an upside-down cake, but will send your punch the other way.

35 to 50 servings

INGREDIENTS

1 FRESH PINEAPPLE, PEELED, CORED, AND SLICED INTO RINGS

6 LEMONS, THINLY SLICED

4 QUARTS WATER

2 750-ML BOTTLES RYE WHISKEY

2 CUPS DARK JAMAICAN RUM

1. Place the pineapple and lemon slices in a large punch bowl. Add the water, rye, and rum. Mix thoroughly, being careful not to break up the pineapple rings.

2. Gently add a large ice block to the punch bowl, and serve.

CHARLESTON LIGHT DRAGOON PUNCH

~ Circa 1852 ~

═══════════════ ⟠ ═══════════════

MANY GREAT PUNCHES have roots in the antebellum South, including this one from the Lowcountry of South Carolina. While this recipe recommends letting the punch sit for four hours, other recipes have called for it to rest for four days. For those in desperate need of a glass of punch, a four-hour rest is clearly preferable. Once perfected, this punch is the ideal refreshment for a small (and jovial) army.

⚭ *40 to 60 servings*

INGREDIENTS

3½ CUPS WATER

1¼ CUPS LEMON JUICE, PEELS RESERVED (ABOUT 8 LEMONS)

2 CUPS ORANGE JUICE, FRESHLY SQUEEZED, PEELS RESERVED (ABOUT 8 ORANGES)

2 GREEN TEA BAGS

⅓ CUP GRENADINE SYRUP

⅓ CUP CURAÇAO OR OTHER ORANGE LIQUEUR

⅓ CUP RASPBERRY SYRUP (SEE PAGE 35)

⅓ CUP CANNED CHERRIES IN SYRUP

⅓ CUP CANNED WHITE CHERRIES

⅓ CUP CANNED SLICED PINEAPPLE

5 CUPS RYE WHISKEY

¾ CUP LIGHT RUM

3 QUARTS SELTZER WATER

1. Combine the water and orange and lemon rinds in a large saucepan set over medium heat. Bring to a boil. Remove the pan from the heat, and add the tea bags. Steep the tea for at least 10 minutes. Let the tea cool before proceeding.

2. In a large bowl, combine the orange and lemon juices, then slowly add the grenadine, Curaçao, and raspberry syrups. Add the green tea while stirring constantly. Add the cherries, pineapple, and any juices that may have collected. Stir thoroughly, then slowly add the rye and rum. Let the punch sit for 4 hours for the flavors to meld.

3. Right before serving, add at least 1½ quarts of seltzer water, and then pour the punch into a large punch bowl that's been filled with ice cubes. If you feel the punch needs further diluting, add more carbonated water, slowly, to taste.

BEETIFUL APPLES

From Gina Chersevani, PS7's, Washington, D.C.

= ᏟᏙᎩᎾ =

STARCHEFS RISING STAR MIXOLOGIST AWARD WINNER Gina Chersevani recently worked closely with PS7's chef/owner Peter Smith to integrate the often-separate worlds of kitchen and bar. The results are sometimes surprising, and always delicious, such as this punch combining a beet reduction and a single malt Scotch.

~ *15 to 22 servings*

INGREDIENTS

½ CUP POWDERED SUGAR (SEE PAGE 34)
1 ¼ CUPS LEMON JUICE (ABOUT 8 LEMONS)
1 750-ML BOTTLE HIGHLAND PARK 12
1 ¼ CUPS DOLIN ROUGE VERMOUTH
4 CUPS APPLE JUICE
1 ¼ CUPS RED BEET REDUCTION
(RECIPE FOLLOWS)
10 DASHES FEE BROTHERS
OLD FASHIONED BITTERS
30 MINT LEAVES
1 TABLESPOON ORANGE ZEST

INGREDIENTS FOR RED BEET REDUCTION

2 MEDIUM-SIZE BEETS, PEELED AND
SLICED
3 CUPS WATER
2 CUPS SUGAR
1 SPLIT VANILLA BEAN

1. In a punch bowl, combine sugar, lemon juice, Highland Park, and vermouth. Whisk until sugar is dissolved. Add apple juice, beet reduction, and the bitters.

2. Add an ice block, and let the mixture stand for about 20 minutes before serving. Garnish each cup with mint leaves and orange zest.

For the Red Beet Reduction

1. In a pot, combine beets, water, sugar, and vanilla bean. Bring the mixture to a boil, then lower heat and allow to simmer for 10 minutes.

2. Remove from heat and allow the mixture to cool. When cool to the touch, strain through a fine mesh sieve, discarding the solids. The liquid is ready to use.

◎◎◎

WEDGEWOOD "OLD VINE" PATTERN DIMINUTIVE PUNCH BOWL ~ CIRCA 1930S
Transfer and hand-colored luster decoration

YELLOWBELLY PUNCH

From Rachel Sergi, Washington, D.C.

〜

WHEN IT WAS REINTRODUCED IN 2008 to the U.S. market after a long absence, Dolin Rouge Vermouth ignited the interest of every bartender and cocktail enthusiast who could find it. Made in France's only appellation for vermouth since 1821, it is distinguished by a fresher, richer taste than the bigger brands of vermouth. The Rouge plays particularly well with the rye in this punch that, thanks to the addition of citrus, tastes a bit like a Manhattan wintering in Miami.

〜 *15 to 20 servings*

INGREDIENTS

- 1 CUP HONEY SYRUP (RECIPE FOLLOWS)
- 2 CUPS GRAPEFRUIT JUICE, FRESHLY SQUEEZED (ABOUT 2 GRAPEFRUITS)
- 2 CUPS TANGERINE JUICE (ABOUT 16 TANGERINES)
- 1 LITER BOTTLE OF JIM BEAM RYE
- 1 375-ML BOTTLE DOLIN ROUGE VERMOUTH
  GRAPEFRUIT BITTERS TO TASTE
- 1 TANGERINE, SLICED
- 1 GRAPEFRUIT, SLICED
  FENNEL FRONDS

INGREDIENTS FOR HONEY SYRUP

- 1 CUP WATER
- 2 CUPS HONEY

1. In the belly of a punch bowl or other large vessel, combine the honey syrup and citrus juice.

2. Add rye, vermouth, and bitters. Stir, then garnish the bowl with slices of tangerine and grapefruit and the fennel fronds. Serve in ice-filled glasses.

For the Honey Syrup

1. Combine water and honey in a medium saucepan over medium-high heat. Bring to a boil, stirring until the honey has dissolved. Reduce the heat to medium-low, and cook for 5 minutes.

2. Cool completely before using or storing in the refrigerator in a tightly sealed glass jar, where it will keep for 2 to 4 weeks.

COTILLION CLUB PUNCH

~ *Circa 1890* ~

══════════════════ ⟨☰☰☰⟩ ══════════════════

WHILE THIS PUNCH may have been created for gatherings of genteel Southern belles, it is far from demure. There was no need to smuggle a flask to the party if this punch was on the menu.

══

~ *24 to 36 servings*

INGREDIENTS

3 ¼ CUPS BOILING WATER
  2 GREEN TEA BAGS
  ⅔ CUP LEMON JUICE (ABOUT 4 LEMONS)
1 ½ 750-ML BOTTLES RYE WHISKEY
  ¼ CUP DARK RUM
  ⅓ CUP SIMPLE SYRUP (SEE PAGE 33)
  ⅔ CUP CANNED CHERRIES, IN SYRUP
  ¼ CUP STRAWBERRY SYRUP (OPTIONAL)
  2 QUARTS SELTZER WATER

1. In a large bowl, pour the boiling water over the green tea bags. Let the tea steep until it is strong. Cool the tea to room temperature.

2. When the brewed tea is cool, add the lemon juice, rye, and rum. Add the simple syrup and cherries with their syrup, and stir well. Add the fruit syrup to sweeten, if desired. Transfer the punch to the refrigerator, and chill for at least 3 hours before serving.

3. When ready to serve, pour the punch over a block of ice that's been set in a punch bowl. Add the seltzer water. Mix thoroughly.

POTENT POTION

~ *Circa 1915* ~

ALTHOUGH IT SOUNDS like it might be a witch's brew, this simple punch is actually a relative of the Manhattan, with its use of rye whiskey, vermouth, and bitters. Use fresh, high-quality vermouth—too often vermouth is left open for months between uses, which significantly alters its taste (and not for the better).

6 to 8 servings

INGREDIENTS

5 TEASPOONS DEMERARA SUGAR
  GRATED ZEST OF HALF A LEMON
1 CUP SWEET VERMOUTH
2 CUPS RYE WHISKEY
1 TEASPOON ANGOSTURA BITTERS
1 CUP WATER

1. Muddle the sugar and the lemon zest together in a mixing bowl. Add the vermouth, rye, and Angostura bitters.

2. Add the water, stir well, and pour into a small punch bowl that has been filled with ice cubes.

MONKEY'S UNCLE PUNCH

From J. P. Caceres, Againn, Washington, D.C.

AT FIRST THE IDEA OF MAKING your own infused spirit or liqueur may seem intimidating but the process is quite simple. It just requires a little forethought. If you've ever made cold-brewed coffee or sun tea, then you've made an infusion. Straining out the materials you've infused can be the most difficult part. Sometimes it's best to use multiple passes through increasingly fine materials. Start with a mesh strainer, and then try cheesecloth or coffee filters. Your patience will be rewarded.

15 to 20 servings

INGREDIENTS

1½ CUPS SPICE-INFUSED BOURBON (RECIPE FOLLOWS)
1 QUART MAGNER'S IRISH CIDER
½ CUP HOMEMADE BANANA LIQUEUR (RECIPE FOLLOWS)
½ CUP LEMON JUICE (ABOUT 3 LEMONS)
¼ TEASPOON GROUND CARDAMOM
15 TO 20 STAR ANISE FOR GARNISH
15 TO 20 ORANGE WHEELS FOR GARNISH (ABOUT 2 ORANGES)

INGREDIENTS FOR SPICE-INFUSED BOURBON

6 CINNAMON STICKS
12 STAR ANISE
1 TABLESPOON ALLSPICE
1 TABLESPOON CARDAMOM
1 TABLESPOON CLOVE
1 375-ML BOTTLE BOURBON

INGREDIENTS FOR BANANA LIQUEUER

1 CUP DARK RUM
2 CUPS LIGHT RUM
2 SPLIT VANILLA BEANS
¼ CUP DARK CHOCOLATE (60% CACAO MINIMUM)
4 SLICED BANANAS

1. Combine all the ingredients in a lidded container. Refrigerate for at least two hours before serving.

2. When ready to serve, add a large block of ice to the bowl, and gently pour in the punch. Garnish the glasses with star anise and orange wheels.

For the Spice-Infused Bourbon

1. In a hot pan, toast cinnamon sticks, star anise, allspice, cardamom, and clove, about 5 minutes. Remove from heat, and let the spices cool.

2. In a sandwich bag or glass jar with a tight-fitting lid, combine the bottle of bourbon and the toasted spices. Keep in a cool, dark place for 7 days. Strain and discard the spices.

For the Banana Liqueur

1. In a large freezer bag or glass jar with a tight-fitting lid, combine dark rum, light rum, vanilla beans, dark chocolate, and bananas.

2. Let the mixture sit in a cool, dark place for 7 days. Strain and discard solids.

DOULTON BURSLEM FOOTED PORCELAIN PUNCH BOWL ~ CIRCA 1880
Hand-painted enamel, Arts and Crafts style floral decoration in
unusual palette of bittersweet orange and green with gold tracery

3.

BRANDY PUNCHES

"Claret is the liquor for boys; port for men;
but he who aspires to be a hero must drink brandy."

—SAMUEL JOHNSON, from
James Boswell's *Life of Samuel Johnson*

HOT MULLED APPLE CIDER AND BRANDY PUNCH

~ Circa 1700 ~

APPLE BRANDY, also known as Applejack, is the oldest liquor made in the United States. Sadly, there is only one major distributor of Applejack left, Laird's, but happily, their product is terrific. Small local distilleries producing apple brandy do exist, and you can always use the legendary French apple brandy, Calvados, as a substitute.

24 to 36 servings

INGREDIENTS

 2 CINNAMON STICKS
15 WHOLE CLOVES
 5 CARDAMOM PODS
 1 GALLON APPLE CIDER
 2 CUPS APPLE BRANDY
12 TO 15 ORANGE SLICES (ABOUT 1 ORANGE)
12 TO 15 APPLE WEDGES (ABOUT 1 APPLE)

1. Put the cinnamon sticks, cloves, and cardamom pods in a square of cheesecloth, and tie the ends closed with kitchen twine.

2. Put the cider in a saucepan set over medium heat, and add the bag of spices. Heat the cider until it just begins to simmer.

3. Remove the pan from the stove, and pour the punch into a punch bowl. Add 1 cup of the apple brandy to the punch; taste the punch and add more apple brandy, if desired. Remove the packet of spices, garnish with orange slices and apple wedges, and serve.

Page 87: ENGLISH ARTS AND CRAFTS PORCELAIN FOOTED PUNCH BOWL (C. 1900), *polychrome enamel decoration in the William Morris style*

BRANDY PUNCH—
AN AMERICAN SENSATION

From Cooling Cups and Dainty Drinks, *1869*

━━━━━━━━━━━━━━━ ✦ ━━━━━━━━━━━━━━━

RASPBERRY SYRUP is easier to whip up than you might think, and it makes a wonderful addition to punches like this one. Substitute grenadine when raspberries are not available for a less fruity, but still delicious, variation.

━━━━━━━━━━━━━━━━━━━━━━━━━━━━━━━━━━

∾ 6 servings

INGREDIENTS

1 CUP WATER
4 TABLESPOONS DEMERARA SUGAR
2 TABLESPOONS RASPBERRY SYRUP
  (SEE PAGE 35)
3 TABLESPOONS LEMON JUICE
  (ABOUT 1 LEMON)
½ CUP ORANGE JUICE, FRESHLY
  SQUEEZED (ABOUT 2 ORANGES)
2 SLICES FRESH PINEAPPLE
1 CUP BRANDY

1. In a medium punch bowl, combine the water, sugar, and raspberry syrup, stirring until the sugar is dissolved.

2. Add the lemon and orange juices and the slice of pineapple. Finally, add the brandy and stir well. Serve in tumblers filled with ice cubes.

GARDEN PARTY PUNCH

From The Ideal Bartender, *1917*

꧁꧂

THE NAME SAYS IT ALL. With the light sweetness of Tokaji (also spelled Tokay or Tokai) or other dessert wine and the herbaceous perfume of monk-made Chartreuse, Garden Party Punch makes for a wonderful springtime sipper. Drop in your favorite herbs—thyme and rosemary are excellent choices—for an even more fragrant concoction.

꧁ *24 to 36 servings*

INGREDIENTS

  6 TABLESPOONS LEMON JUICE
    (ABOUT 2 LEMONS)

  3 TABLESPOONS ORANGE JUICE, FRESHLY
    SQUEEZED (ABOUT ⅓ OF AN ORANGE)

1⅔ CUPS DEMERARA SUGAR

  3 TABLESPOONS GREEN CHARTREUSE

  2 CUPS BRANDY

  3 750-ML BOTTLES TOKAJI, SAUTERNES
    OR OTHER WHITE DESSERT WINE

  1 750-ML BOTTLE BORDEAUX OR OTHER
    FULL-BODIED RED WINE

15 TO 20 ORANGE SLICES
    (ABOUT 2 ORANGES)

10 TO 15 LEMON SLICES (ABOUT 2 LEMONS)

1. Place a large block of ice into a large punch bowl.

2. In a separate bowl, combine the lemon and orange juices and the sugar, stirring until the sugar is dissolved. Add the mixture to the punch bowl. While stirring slowly, add the Chartreuse and brandy.

3. Add the Tokaji and the red wine, and stir well. Serve in wine glasses garnished with a slice of orange or lemon.

CAROUSEL PUNCH

From The Bon Vivants, San Francisco, California

======= ◦∞◦ =======

TRADITIONAL ENGLISH PIMM'S NO. 1 is a complex mixture that, on its own, is almost a punch in a bottle. It only needs its frequent companion, lemonade, to create an even older, and equally beloved, drink. Here, Pimm's blend of gin, quinine, and herbs mingles with a complex array of ingredients that will leave your palate feeling quite merry.

∾ 18 to 26 servings

INGREDIENTS

- 60 POMEGRANATE SEEDS
- 1 750-ML BOTTLE CALVADOS
- 1 750-ML BOTTLE PIMM'S
- 1 ¾ CUPS LEMON JUICE (ABOUT 10 LEMONS)
- 1 ¼ CUPS POMEGRANATE JUICE
- 1 ¾ CUPS UNFILTERED APPLE JUICE
- 2 ¼ CUPS FIVE-SPICE HONEY SYRUP (RECIPE FOLLOWS)
- 2 TABLESPOONS FEE BROTHERS WHISKEY BARREL BITTERS
- 2 TABLESPOONS PEYCHAUD'S BITTERS
- 20 APPLE SLICES (ABOUT 1½ APPLES)

INGREDIENTS FOR FIVE-SPICE HONEY SYRUP

- 4 STAR ANISE
- 20 CLOVES
- 6 CINNAMON STICKS
- 5 CRACKED NUTMEGS
- 12 ALLSPICE BERRIES
- 2 ¼ CUPS HONEY
- ¾ CUP WATER

1. The day before serving, distribute pomegranate seeds among 6 double rocks glasses. Add water to each glass and freeze.

2. Combine all the liquid ingredients in a punch bowl, stirring until the ingredients are assimilated. Add 20 thin slices of apple, cut perpendicular to the core to allow for the star shape surrounding the seeds to be exposed. Add the pomegranate ice cubes to the punch just before serving.

For the Five-Spice Honey Syrup

1. In a cast-iron skillet or other heavy-bottomed pan over medium heat, toast spices until lightly browned and aromatic, about 2 to 5 minutes, tossing frequently.

2. In a saucepan, combine honey, water, and toasted spices. Simmer for 10 minutes on medium heat to extract spice oils.

3. Strain out the solids, and cool the mixture before using.

Furnivals Aesthetic Movement Punch Bowl ~ Circa 1890
Scalloped rim and all-over hibiscus floral pattern

LEGARE STREET PUNCH

~ Circa 1890 ~

═══════════════ ⚬ ═══════════════

NAMED FOR THE FAMOUS THOROUGHFARE in the historic portion of Charleston, South Carolina, this light and refreshing punch is the perfect drink for breezy early summer evenings. If Champagne is outside your budget, substitute Cava, Prosecco, or other traditional-method sparkling wine.

~ 15 to 20 servings

INGREDIENTS

2 CUPS SAUTERNES, OR OTHER DESSERT WINE
1 CUP COGNAC
1 750-ML BOTTLE CHAMPAGNE
2 CUPS SELTZER WATER

1. Combine the Sauternes and the cognac in a large mixing bowl. Add the Champagne and carbonated water, stirring slowly and gently so as not to break up the bubbles.

2. Fill a large punch bowl halfway with ice cubes, and slowly pour the punch over the ice. Serve immediately.

TRADD ALLEY PUNCH

~ Circa 1890 ~

———————————————— ⟲〰〰〰⟳ ————————————————

THIS DELICIOUS PUNCH FROM THE LOWCOUNTRY is an irresistable crowd pleaser, with its potent array of different liquors offset by the sweet counterpoint of the maraschino cherries.

———————————————————————————————————————

➤ *15 to 20 servings*

INGREDIENTS

2 750-ML BOTTLES SHERRY
1 CUP BRANDY
1 CUP DARK RUM
4 TABLESPOONS DEMERARA SUGAR
⅓ CUP LEMON JUICE (ABOUT 2 LEMONS)
1 10-OUNCE JAR MARASCHINO CHERRIES,
   WITH JUICE
   SELTZER

1. Combine the sherry, brandy, and rum in a large mixing bowl. Add the sugar, and stir until dissolved. Add the lemon juice and the maraschino cherries with the juice.

2. Place a large block of ice in a punch bowl, and gently pour the punch into the bowl. If desired, add seltzer to taste.

AT-HOME PISCO PUNCH

From Duggan McDonnell, Cantina, San Francisco, California

PISCO, A BRANDY that has been made in Peru and Chile for centuries, was wildly popular in eighteenth-century San Francisco. Travelers from the East who sailed to California had to sail around South America, stocking up on the spirit during the journey. Once the Pisco arrived in San Francisco, it found its way into many punch recipes. One of the most popular versions of Pisco Punch was served at the Bank Exchange saloon, but the owner supposedly took the recipe, and a much-conjectured-about secret ingredient, with him to the grave. Modern punchmaster Duggan McDonnell offers a contemporary recipe.

~ *15 servings*

INGREDIENTS

1 WHOLE PINEAPPLE

2 CUPS WATER

1 CUP LIGHT BROWN SUGAR

1 TEASPOON GROUND CINNAMON POWDER

1 CUP LIME JUICE (ABOUT 8 LIMES)

2 CUPS RICHLY STEEPED GREEN TEA

3 ORANGES, PEELED IN A LONG STRIP

1 LEMON, PEELED IN A LONG STRIP

1 750-ML BOTTLE CAMPO DE ENCANTO PISCO DE PERU

6 CINNAMON STICKS

SELTZER

1. Slice the skin away from the pineapple in long strokes, being careful to keep a minimum of fruit along the interior of the skin. Place the skins in a small pot, and add the water. Simmer on low heat for one hour.

2. Remove the pineapple skins, and add the sugar and the cinnamon powder, stirring thoroughly. Remove the mixture from the heat.

3. Juice the pineapple in a blender or commercial juicer, and then add the lime juice. Strain out the pulp.

4. In a large bowl, combine the fruit juice and cinnamon-pineapple syrup.

5. Brew the rich green tea, allow to steep, then add it to the mixture.

6. Pour the bottle of Campo de Encanto and the pineapple-juice-syrup-green-tea mixture into a punch bowl. Add the citrus peels and the cinnamon sticks. Squeeze the oranges and lemon for their juice into the punch, add ice, and stir thoroughly. Add a bit of seltzer water for pep just before serving.

WEST INDIES PUNCH

Adapted from *Trader Vic's Bartender's Guide*, 1946

This simple but delicious punch conjures up hot summer days, offering the perfect balance of heft and zing. Madeira is a fortified wine often used in cooking, but don't even think of using cooking wine for this summertime quencher. The standard rule for any spirit or wine used in punch: Do not add it if you are not willing to drink a glass of it.

18 and 26 servings

INGREDIENTS

 2 GREEN TEA BAGS
 2 CUPS WATER, HEATED TO 150 TO 160°F
 2 CUPS DEMERARA SUGAR
1½ CUPS LIME JUICE (ABOUT 12 LIMES)
12 LIME RINDS
 1 CUP GUAVA MARMALADE
1⅔ CUP DARK JAMAICAN RUM
1⅔ CUP LIGHT RUM
 2 CUPS COGNAC
 1 750-ML BOTTLE MADEIRA

1. Pour the hot water into a large bowl, and add the tea bags. Let steep for at least 5 minutes and up to 10 minutes. Add the lime juice and rinds.

2. In a saucepan set over high heat, bring 2 cups of water to a boil. Add the guava marmalade, and stir until dissolved.

3. Pour the marmalade mixture into the tea mixture. Add the dark and light rums, cognac, and wine. Stir well.

4. Transfer the bowl to the refrigerator, and chill for at least 4 hours.

5. Remove the lime rinds from the bowl, and pour the punch over a large block of ice that has been set in a punch bowl.

ENGLISH ARTS AND CRAFTS PORCELAIN FOOTED PUNCH BOWL ~ CIRCA 1900
Polychrome enamel decoration in the William Morris style

DIABLO'S PUNCH

Adapted from a recipe by Milo Rodriguez, Miami, Florida

PASSIONFRUIT JUICE gives this punch a sensual, tropical flavor. Different brands have different amounts of sweetness, so if you can't find Rubicon (available in some specialty groceries), add sugar to the juice you *can* find, to taste. You can also make your own from fresh passionfruit. Choose ripe fruit (they are wrinkled when ripe). Slice the fruit in half, scrape out the pulp, place it in a blender with about 1½ cups of water and 1 teaspoon of sugar, and blend using a low setting so as not to break the seeds. Strain the mixture, and add more sugar or water to taste.

15 to 20 servings

INGREDIENTS

1 750-ML BOTTLE LA DIABLADA PISCO

1¼ CUPS TAYLOR'S VELVET FALERNUM OR HOMEMADE FALERNUM SYRUP (SEE PAGE 35)

3⅛ CUPS RUBICON PASSIONFRUIT JUICE

1 CUP LIME JUICE, STRAINED (ABOUT 8 LIMES)

½ 750-ML BOTTLE GOOD-QUALITY ROSÉ CHAMPAGNE

1 LIME, SLICED

30 TO 40 MINT LEAVES

1. Combine Pisco, falernum, passionfruit juice, and lime juice. Stir well.

2. Pour over a large ice block set in a punch bowl. Stir and top with Champagne. Garnish the bowl with the lime slices. Garnish each cup with 1 or 2 mint leaves.

DOUBLE SPICE PUNCH

From David Lanzalone, POV at the W Hotel, Washington, D.C.

SPICE IS ONE OF THE FIVE ESSENTIAL ELEMENTS of punch. Nowadays, you can conveniently choose from a number of different rums that already have spice added. This punch calls not only for spiced rum, but also for spiced syrup. Layering the flavors this way creates a more complex drink. Another way to add complexity to a punch is to use multiple spirits. This recipe combines two very different rums with a rich, aged cognac, creating a sensational concoction that's hard to figure out and equally hard to put down.

45 to 65 servings

INGREDIENTS

- 1 750-ML BOTTLE RÉMY MARTIN V.S.O.P. COGNAC
- 1 750-ML BOTTLE APPLETON VX RUM
- 1 750-ML BOTTLE KRAKEN DARK SPICED RUM
- 1 GALLON APPLE CIDER
- 3⅛ CUPS LEMON JUICE (ABOUT 18 LEMONS)
- 1 CUP QUINCE JELLY
- 3 CUPS SPICED SYRUP (RECIPE FOLLOWS)
- 45 TO 65 APPLE SLICES (ABOUT 6 APPLES)

INGREDIENTS FOR SPICED SYRUP

- 1½ CUPS DEMERARA SUGAR
- 1½ CUPS HOT WATER
- ¼ CUP MAPLE SYRUP
- ½ TABLESPOON GROUND ALLSPICE
- 2 CINNAMON STICKS
- 25 WHOLE CLOVES

1. Combine ingredients in a punch bowl.

2. Stir until jelly is dissolved, then add an ice block, and stir again. Garnish with apple slices.

For the Spiced Syrup

1. Dissolve sugar in hot water. Add maple syrup, allspice, cinnamon sticks, and whole cloves to a container with a tight-fitting lid.

2. Allow spices to infuse overnight, and then strain out the solids before using or storing in a glass jar with a tight-fitting lid.

Royal Doulton Arts and Crafts Footed Punch Bowl ~ Circa 1910
Decorated with all-over poppy transfer decoration and polychrome enamel

4.

GIN PUNCHES

"For gin, in cruel
Sober truth,
Supplies the fuel
For flaming youth."

—Noel Coward,
English actor and playwright, 1899–1973

GIN PUNCH À LA TERRINGTON

From Cooling Cups and Dainty Drinks, *1869*

GROUNDBREAKING MIXOLOGIST, punch maker, and author William Terrington created this simple gin punch in the mid-nineteenth century. In its short list of ingredients, it embodies punch's fivefold nature, with the "spice" note provided by the wonderfully herbal Chartreuse.

~ *15 to 20 servings*

INGREDIENTS

GRATED ZEST OF ½ LEMON

½ CUP DEMERARA SUGAR

½ CUP LEMON JUICE (ABOUT 3 LEMONS)

2 CUPS GIN

¾ CUP CHARTREUSE

1 TO 2 QUARTS SELTZER WATER

1. In a large bowl, muddle the lemon zest and sugar with a wooden spoon. Add the lemon juice, and stir well. Add the gin and Chartreuse.

2. Fill a small punch bowl with ice cubes, and pour the punch over the ice.

3. Add 1 quart of the seltzer, and stir gently. If the punch tastes too strong, add more seltzer.

Page 105: VILLEROY AND BOCH FOOTED PUNCH BOWL (c. 1920), *blue and white transfer featuring all-over landscapes, Germany*

GIN PUNCH

From The Dessert Book, *1872*

THE BELOVED COCKTAIL known as the Tom Collins started its life as a punch—a gin punch, of course. In this light and refreshing concoction, the addition of maraschino liqueur and citrus zest provide a bright counterpoint to the juniper notes in the gin. For a variation on the theme, try Plymouth or Old Tom Gin, or even Genever, in place of London Dry Gin.

15 to 20 servings

INGREDIENTS

- 1 CUP LONDON DRY GIN
  GRATED ZEST OF 1 LEMON
- 2 TABLESPOONS LEMON JUICE
  (ABOUT ½ OF A LEMON)
- 1 CUP WATER
- ½ CUP MARASCHINO LIQUEUR
- 2 TABLESPOONS DEMERARA SUGAR
- 2 QUARTS SELTZER WATER
- 15 TO 20 THIN SLICES OF LEMON RIND
  (ABOUT 2 LEMONS)

1. In a medium punch bowl, combine the gin, lemon zest, and lemon juice. Add the water and maraschino liqueur, then add the sugar. Stir well, transfer the bowl to the refrigerator, and chill for at least 2 hours.

2. To serve, remove the bowl from the refrigerator, and pour in the seltzer. Serve the punch in lowball glasses filled with ice cubes and garnished with a thin slice of lemon rind.

CHIP SHOP PUNCH

From Jake Parrot, Ledroit Brands, Washington, D.C.

BEEFEATER LONDON DRY GIN stands in for brandy in this crisp variation on the Colonial-era Fish House Punch. Though inspired by the losing side of the Revolutionary War, it's the unexpected zing of a product of another onetime British colony—Jamaica's Coruba rum—that really ties this punch together.

12 to 18 servings

INGREDIENTS

- 1 750-ML BOTTLE BEEFEATER GIN
- 1 CUP ROTHMAN & WINTER APRICOT LIQUEUR
- ½ CUP CORUBA RUM
- 1 CUP LEMON JUICE (ABOUT 6 LEMONS)
- 1 CUP SIMPLE SYRUP (SEE PAGE 33)
- 2⅔ CUPS WATER
- 2 TEASPOONS ANGOSTURA BITTERS

1. Combine ingredients in a large container.

2. Pour the mixture over an ice block set in a punch bowl and stir to chill.

CHATHAM ARTILLERY PUNCH

~ Circa 1860 ~

CHATHAM ARTILLERY is the oldest U.S. regiment from Georgia, still active under the 1st Battalion of the 118th Field Artillery Regiment. This punch is as potent as its namesake and has probably laid low as many soldiers over the years. According to a 1930s article in *The New York Herald Tribune*, "This is the punch that knocked out Admiral Schley when he visited Savannah in 1899 after the Spanish War. Admiral Cervera's Spanish shells were harmless to the brave American admiral, but Artillery Punch scored a direct hit which put him out for two days."

~ 40 to 60 servings

INGREDIENTS

1½ 750-ML BOTTLES ROSÉ WINE
1 750-ML BOTTLE DARK RUM
3 CUPS COLD WATER
2 CUPS GIN
2 CUPS RYE WHISKEY
2 CUPS BRANDY
¼ POUND PINEAPPLE, SLICED
1¼ CUPS LIGHT BROWN SUGAR
1 CUP MARASCHINO CHERRIES, WITH JUICE
1¾ CUPS LEMON JUICE (ABOUT 5 LEMONS)
2 GREEN TEA BAGS
3 TO 5 750 ML BOTTLES CHAMPAGNE

1. In a large container that has a tightly fitting lid, combine the wine, rum, water, gin, rye whiskey, brandy, pineapple, sugar, cherries, lemon juice, and tea bags. Cover and store the punch in a cool, dark place for a minimum of 24 hours (the original recipe suggests 2 months!), so that all the ingredients can blend.

2. To serve, pour the mixture into a large punch bowl that has been filled with ice cubes. Add at least one bottle of Champagne, and stir gently. If you would like to make the punch stronger, add more Champagne to the bowl before serving.

VILLEROY AND BOCH FOOTED PUNCH BOWL ~ CIRCA 1890
Blue and white transfer featuring all-over landscapes, Germany

HORSE AND CARRIAGE PUNCH

From Simon Ford, Pernod-Ricard, New York, New York

YOU MAY THINK OF CHAMOMILE TEA as a cozy brew best sipped right before bedtime, but along with its well-known use as a sleep aid it has been used to treat a variety of ailments over the ages. Chamomile's restorative properties probably account for how it found its way into so many recipes for liqueurs and bitters over the centuries. Here it joins floral forces with St. Germain to balance the juniper bite of Plymouth Gin and the effervescent acidity of Champagne to form the sort of punch you can imagine soothing yourself with on a sunny afternoon.

20 to 30 servings

INGREDIENTS

    5 ORANGES, PEELED; PEELS SLICED
      INTO THIN STRIPS
    5 LEMONS, PEELED; PEELS SLICED
      INTO THIN STRIPS
    1 CUP FINE WHITE SUGAR (SEE PAGE 34)
    1 750-ML BOTTLE PLYMOUTH GIN
 2⅓ CUPS ST. GERMAIN ELDERFLOWER
      LIQUEUR
 3⅛ CUPS CHAMOMILE TEA
 1⅔ CUPS LEMON JUICE (ABOUT 10 LEMONS)
  ¾ CUP SOLERNO BLOOD ORANGE LIQUEUR
  ⅓ CUP GOLDEN HONEY SYRUP
      (RECIPE FOLLOWS)
    1 750-ML BOTTLE PERRIER-JOUËT
      CHAMPAGNE
    1 ORANGE, SLICED
    1 LEMON, SLICED
      ELDERBERRIES, OPTIONAL

INGREDIENTS FOR GOLDEN HONEY SYRUP

  ⅓ CUP WATER
  ⅔ CUP HONEY

1. In a punch bowl, muddle the orange and lemon peels with the sugar. Add the next 6 ingredients, stirring to combine.

2. Add ice cubes, and top the punch with chilled Champagne. Garnish with orange and lemon slices and elderberries, if using.

For the Golden Honey Syrup
1. Combine water and honey in a medium saucepan over medium-high heat. Bring to a boil, stirring until the honey has dissolved. Reduce the heat to medium-low, and cook for 5 minutes.

2. Cool completely before using or storing in the refrigerator in a tightly sealed glass jar, where it will keep for 2 to 4 weeks.

DRY GIN PUNCH

~ Circa 1915 ~

━━━━━━━━━━━━━━━━━ ◦ⱲⱲ◦ ━━━━━━━━━━━━━━━━━

WHAT MAKES THIS PUNCH DRY is the use of London Dry Gin. If you can't lay your hands on London Dry Gin, make sure to choose something with a similarly strong juniper profile, which provides the counterpoint to the sweet orange juice.

━━━━━━━━━━━━━━━━━━━━━━━━━━━━━━━━━━━━━━━

18 to 24 servings

INGREDIENTS

- 1 QUART ORANGE JUICE, FRESHLY SQUEEZED (ABOUT 16 ORANGES)
- ¾ CUP LEMON JUICE (ABOUT 5 LEMONS)
- ¼ CUP PLUS 2 TABLESPOONS GRENADINE
- 3 CUPS LONDON DRY GIN
- 1 QUART SELTZER WATER
- 2 LEMONS, SLICED
- 1 ORANGE, SLICED

1. Pour the orange juice, lemon juice, and grenadine into a large bowl, and stir well. Slowly add the gin, and stir well.

2. Transfer the bowl to the refrigerator, and chill for 2 hours.

3. To serve, pour the punch over a block of ice that has been set in a large punch bowl. Add the seltzer water, and stir gently. Garnish the punch with the fruit slices.

SOYER'S GIN PUNCH

~ Circa 1915 ~

MOST RECIPES FOR SOYER'S GIN PUNCH include seltzer water with a little mineral content. This one calls simply for water, which is perfectly fine. But if you'd like to add a little savory complexity to the punch, try Apollonaris or Gerolsteiner sparkling water instead.

~ 8 to 12 servings

INGREDIENTS

½ CUP SIMPLE SYRUP (SEE PAGE 33)

⅓ CUP LEMON JUICE (ABOUT 2 LEMONS)

ZEST FROM ½ A LEMON

1 CUP GIN

3 TABLESPOONS MARASCHINO LIQUEUR

1 QUART WATER

1 LEMON, SLICED

1. Mix the simple syrup, lemon juice, and lemon zest together in a large punch bowl. Add the gin and maraschino liqueur, and stir to combine.

2. Add the water, transfer the bowl to the refrigerator, and chill for at least 2 hours.

3. Remove the bowl from the refrigerator. Serve in small punch glasses garnished with a slice of lemon.

THE FLOWING BOLS

From Marcos Tello, The Varnish, Los Angeles, California

⟨⟩

DON'T MAKE THE MISTAKE of thinking of Genever as just another Dutch gin. Though flavored with juniper like other gins, it's more akin to the London Dry style. Genever's most distinctive quality is that it's made with malt wine rather than neutral spirit, so it has a pronounced malty flavor. Mixologists often like to treat it more like a whiskey in cocktails as a result.

10 to 15 servings

INGREDIENTS

2 FRESH PINEAPPLE RINGS

3 LEMON PEELS, THINLY SLICED

3 HEAPING BAR SPOONS OF SUPERFINE WHITE SUGAR (SEE PAGE 34)

¾ CUP RASPBERRY SYRUP (SEE PAGE 35)

¼ CUP MARASCHINO LIQUEUR

⅔ CUP REGAN'S ORANGE BITTERS No. 6

¾ CUP LEMON JUICE (ABOUT 5 LEMONS)

¼ CUP ORANGE JUICE (ABOUT 1 ORANGE)

2 CUPS BOLS GENEVER

1½ CUPS SELTZER WATER

1. Muddle the pineapple rings and lemon peels with the sugar.

2. Add the remaining ingredients, except seltzer water, and stir until the sugar has dissolved. Add some ice cubes, and stir again.

3. Strain over a large block of ice that has been set in a punch bowl. Top with seltzer soda.

⌒௸

Pairpoint Hand-Blown Cobalt Crystal Footed Grape Juice Bowl ~ Circa 1920s
Copper wheel engraved "Vintage" pattern

NUT PUNCH

From Dan Searing, Room 11, Washington, D.C.

THIS PUNCH WAS DEVELOPED with a house-made Vin de Noix, a fortified wine flavored with green walnuts and baking spices. The Nux Alpina Walnut Liqueur from Haus Alpenz is a perfect fit, however, because it is a little lighter than a homemade Nocino, which is another name for this liqueur. If you have to use a different gin, make sure it is another "New Western Dry" gin, or any one of the relatively recent group on the market that dials back the juniper and lets other, sometimes nontraditional botanicals, play a larger role in the flavor.

12 to 18 servings

INGREDIENTS

    1 750-ML BOTTLE OF HENDRICK'S GIN
1 ⅓ CUPS SIMPLE SYRUP (SEE PAGE 33)
    1 CUP NUX ALPINA WALNUT LIQUEUR
    1 CUP LEMON JUICE (ABOUT 6 LEMONS)
2 ⅔ CUPS WATER
   17 DASHES GRAPEFRUIT BITTERS
   30 to 40 SMALL PINK ROSE PETALS
        (ABOUT 5 TEA ROSES)

1. Combine all ingredients in a large, lidded container. Cover and refrigerate until chilled.

2. Pour the mixture over an ice block set in a large punch bowl. Garnish the bowl and cups with small pink rose petals.

5.

WINE PUNCHES

"Samuel Johnson said that few people had intellectual resources sufficient to forgo the pleasures of wine. They could not otherwise contrive how to fill the interval between dinner and supper."

—from James Boswell's
Life of Samuel Johnson

GOTHIC PUNCH

From Jerry Thomas' Bartenders Guide: How to Mix Drinks, *1862*

⟨⟨⟨⟩⟩⟩

THIS IS A SIMPLE, delicious punch and a great recipe for those who are daunted by more labor-intensive, ingredient-heavy punch recipes. Its gothic nature is suggested not only by its provenance, but also by the deep burgundy color reminiscent of the heavy velvet curtains once used to keep drafty stone mansions warm.

⟨⟩ *24 to 36 servings*

INGREDIENTS

  4 750-ML BOTTLES CATAWBA OR OTHER
    SWEET WINE
  1 750-ML BOTTLE BORDEAUX OR
    OTHER FULL-BODIED RED WINE
  ½ CUP PLUS 2 TABLESPOONS FINE
    DEMERARA SUGAR (SEE PAGE 34)
  ¾ CUP ORANGE JUICE (ABOUT 3 ORANGES)
  1 750-ML BOTTLE CHAMPAGNE

1. In a large punch bowl, combine the sweet wine, red wine, and sugar, stirring until the sugar is dissolved. Add the orange juice, and stir well.

2. Chill the mixture for at least 2 hours. To serve, add the Champagne, and stir gently.

Page 121: DOULTON BURSLEM AESTHETIC MOVEMENT PUNCH BOWL (c. 1880), *all-over two-color blue enamel ground with "Japonesque" motif gold overlay*

BEAUFORT PUNCH

From The Dessert Book, *1872*

THIS IS A GREAT SPRING PUNCH that begs to be served outdoors. To really showcase the punch, reserve the ingredients used to flavor the simple syrup and freeze them into a block of ice. Just before you serve, remove the block of ice from the freezer and float it in the bowl.

15 to 20 servings

INGREDIENTS

1 CUP SIMPLE SYRUP (SEE PAGE 33)
½ CUCUMBER, THINLY SLICED
1 BUNCH FRESH LEMON BALM
1 BUNCH TENDER BORAGE LEAVES
6 LEAVES LEMON VERBENA
2 750-ML BOTTLES SAUTERNES
1 QUART SELTZER WATER
1 CUP PINEAPPLE JUICE
1 CUP ORANGE JUICE, FRESHLY SQUEEZED (ABOUT 4 ORANGES)
¼ CUP CURAÇAO OR OTHER ORANGE LIQUEUR

1. Pour the simple syrup into a pitcher, and add the cucumber slices, lemon balm, borage leaves, and verbena. Stir well, and let the mixture steep for 2 hours in the refrigerator.

2. Pour the Sauternes, seltzer water, pineapple juice, orange juice, and Curaçao into a large bowl that has been iced or kept in a freezer until very cold.

3. Strain the infused simple syrup into the bowl, and discard the solids. Transfer the bowl to the refrigerator, and chill for no less than 30 minutes. Serve in lowball glasses over ice cubes, if desired.

CONQUISTADOR PUNCH

From Dan Searing, Room 11, Washington, D.C.

In 1933, Jerez, where the famous fortified wine known as sherry is produced, became the first protected Denominación de Origen in Spain. Centuries earlier, the Spanish brought the distilling knowledge used to make the brandy that fortifies sherry to Mexico, and tequila was the eventual result. Conquistador Punch was inspired by colonial-era Spain's attempt to subjugate Mexico. The colonialism ultimately failed, but it did inspire a blending of the two cultures. In this punch, sweet Spanish sherry harmonizes with spicy Mexican tequila, mirroring the efforts of the conquistadors and creating a new flavor all its own.

~ 12 to 18 servings

INGREDIENTS

1 750-ML BOTTLE REPOSADO TEQUILA
1 375-ML BOTTLE PEDRO XIMÉNEZ SHERRY
1½ CUPS LIME JUICE (ABOUT 12 LIMES)
1½ CUPS CLEMENTINE JUICE (ABOUT 12 CLEMENTINES)
1 CUP CLEMENTINE ZEST SYRUP (RECIPE FOLLOWS)
1 ICE BLOCK
2 CLEMENTINES, PEELED; PEEL CUT INTO SMALL, COIN SHAPES

INGREDIENTS FOR CLEMENTINE ZEST SYRUP

ZEST FROM 2 CLEMENTINES
1 CUP COLD SIMPLE SYRUP (SEE PAGE 33)

1. Combine all liquid ingredients in a large pitcher, adding the clementine syrup last and to taste. Chill thoroughly. When ready to serve, place the ice block in a punch bowl, and pour the punch over it.

2. Float the clementine slices in the punch. Garnish each serving with small coins of clementine peel gently squeezed over the glass.

For the Clementine Zest Syrup

1. Use a microplane grater to remove the zest from 2 clementines. Add the zest to cold simple syrup.

2. Cover and refrigerate overnight or for up to 24 hours. Strain out the zest. Refrigerate any unused syrup.

BORDEAUX RED WINE PUNCH

From Jerry Thomas' Bartenders Guide: How to Mix Drinks, *1862*

THIS PUNCH IS DIFFERENT from the Cold Claret Punch (see page 128) because it is less fruit-driven and therefore showcases the wine more effectively. Due to its rich, dark flavor, it is best enjoyed during the fall and winter.

18 to 26 servings

INGREDIENTS

1 750-ML BOTTLE BORDEAUX OR OTHER FULL-BODIED RED WINE

¾ CUP SWEET SHERRY

½ CUP BRANDY

4 TABLESPOONS POWDERED SUGAR (SEE PAGE 34)

¼ TEASPOON FRESHLY GRATED NUTMEG

1 LEMON, THINLY SLICED

2 QUARTS SELTZER WATER

1. In a large container with a lid, combine the wine, sherry, brandy, sugar, nutmeg, and lemon slices. Put the container in the refrigerator, and chill for at least 3 hours.

2. To serve, pour the mixture over a block of ice that has been set in a punch bowl. Slowly stir the punch while adding the seltzer.

COLD CLARET PUNCH

From Chafing Dish Recipes, *1896*

CLARET IS THE BRITISH TERM for Bordeaux wine, which is generally a blend of Cabernet Sauvignon, Merlot, and Cabernet Franc along with a few other varietals. In the United States the blend is known as Meritage. If you cannot easily put your hands on either, your best bet is to select a jammy, full-bodied wine.

10 to 15 servings

INGREDIENTS

- 1 750-ML BOTTLE CLARET, OR OTHER BORDEAUX-STYLE FULL-BODIED RED WINE
- ¾ CUP DEMERARA SUGAR
- 2 TABLESPOONS CURAÇAO OR OTHER ORANGE LIQUEUR
- 2 TABLESPOONS KIRSCH
- 2 CUPS COLD WATER
- 3 TABLESPOONS LEMON JUICE (ABOUT 1 LEMON)
- ½ PINT CHERRIES, PITTED, OR PRESERVED CHERRIES

1. Pour the Claret into a medium punch bowl, and add the sugar, Curaçao, and kirsch. Stir well. Add the water and the lemon juice, and stir well.

2. Add the cherries, and float a large block of ice in the punch bowl. Let stand for 15 minutes to chill, then serve.

BISHOP PUNCH

From Cooling Cups and Dainty Drinks, *1869*

━━━━━━━━━━━━━━━━━━━ ⟋⟍⟋ ━━━━━━━━━━━━━━━━━━━

PERFECT FOR HEATING UP a cold day, this is a mulled wine punch much like *glühwein* or *glögg*. Regardless of whether you use lemon or orange zest, try sprinkling freshly grated nutmeg over the punch before ladling it into the glasses.

～ *4 to 6 servings*

INGREDIENTS

1 750-ML BOTTLE TAWNY PORT

½ CUP PLUS 1 TABLESPOON DEMERARA
   SUGAR

6 WHOLE CLOVES

   THINLY SLICED ZEST OF 1 ORANGE OR
   1 LEMON

1. Combine the port, sugar, cloves, and orange or lemon zest in a medium saucepan set over medium heat. Gradually heat the mixture, and remove it from the heat just before it begins to boil.

2. Strain into a punch bowl, and serve.

GLÖGG

From Dina Passman, Washington, D.C.

WHAT WINTER SEASON is complete without a glass of hot spiced wine? Called *glögg* (pronounced "glug") in Scandinavian countries, it's found wherever there is cold weather and red wine. What distinguishes glögg from *glühwein*, as its known to German speakers, or from mulled wine as the English call it, or from wassail (which can also be beer- or cider-based)? In this recipe it's cardamom that sets it apart (green or black can be used). Every tradition has a slightly different take on both the spices as well as the fortifying agent that can be used in the drink, such as aquavit, brandy, rum, port, or Madeira. But as nineteenth-century author Mrs. Beeton wrote in her mulled wine recipe, "it is very difficult to give the exact proportions of ingredients like sugar and spice, as what quantity might suit one person would be to another quite distasteful." So while this recipe is a winner, always remember to let your own palate be your guide.

8 to 12 servings

INGREDIENTS

- 3 CARDAMOM PODS
- 2 750-ML BOTTLES RED WINE
- 1 CINNAMON STICK
- 6 WHOLE CLOVES
- ¾ CUP DEMERARA SUGAR
- ¼ CUP VODKA
- ½ CUP BLANCHED ALMONDS
- ½ CUP RAISINS

1. Using the flat side of a knife, carefully smash the cardamom pods, reserving the shells and seeds.

2. In a large pot set over medium heat, mix the wine, cinnamon stick, cloves, and cardamom pieces. Simmer 5 minutes, then turn off the heat, and let the mixture steep for at least 2 hours. Strain, if desired.

3. Return pot to a low simmer, then slowly add the sugar, stirring constantly. Turn off the heat and stir in the vodka.

4. To serve, put a scant tablespoon each of almonds and raisins into a mug, then pour 6 ounces of glögg on top. Serve with a teaspoon so revelers can eat the almonds and raisins as they drink.

DOULTON BURSLEM AESTHETIC MOVEMENT PUNCH BOWL ~ CIRCA 1880

All-over two-color blue enamel ground with "Japonesque" motif gold overlay

COUNTRY CLUB PUNCH

From The Ideal Bartender, *1917*

======================= ⟨∿⟩ =======================

THIS PUNCH CALLS FOR CHÂTEAU MARGAUX in the recipe that appears in Tom Bullock's *The Ideal Bartender*, but unless you actually belong to a country club (or have serious money of your own to burn) many more affordable Bordeaux wines will do perfectly well.

◦ *50 to 75 servings*

INGREDIENTS

1⅔ CUPS DEMERARA SUGAR

ZEST OF 2 LEMONS

ZEST OF 1 ORANGE

6 ORANGES, SLICED

½ PINEAPPLE, PEELED, CORED, AND SLICED

½ PINT STRAWBERRIES, SLICED

1 QUART SELTZER WATER

2 TABLESPOONS BENEDICTINE

2 TABLESPOONS CURAÇAO OR OTHER ORANGE LIQUEUR

2 TABLESPOONS MARASCHINO LIQUEUR

2 TABLESPOONS JAMAICAN DARK RUM

2 CUPS BRANDY

1 750-ML BOTTLE TOKAJI, CATAWBA, OR OTHER SWEET WINE

1 750-ML BOTTLE MADEIRA

2 750-ML BOTTLES BORDEAUX OR OTHER FULL-BODIED RED WINE

3 750-ML BOTTLES CHAMPAGNE

1. In a large mixing bowl, muddle the sugar with the lemon and orange zest with a wooden spoon. Add the orange slices, pineapple slices, strawberries, and seltzer water.

2. While stirring slowly, add the Benedictine, Curaçao, maraschino liqueur, and rum.

3. Strain the mixture into a very large punch bowl that has been filled with ice cubes. Add the brandy, sweet wine, Madeira, and red wine. Add the Champagne, and serve. Garnish each glass with the fruits and berries from the punch bowl.

CLUB HOUSE PUNCH

From The Ideal Bartender, *1917*

WHILE EUROPE is known for its grape varietals, the United States has a few of its own, including the Catawba, a grape that has been widely grown along the East Coast since the nineteenth century. Henry Wadsworth Longfellow praised the lightly sweet, rosé-colored Catawba wine in the poem "Catawba Wine":

> *While pure as a spring*
> *Is the wine I sing,*
> *And to praise it, one needs but name it;*
> *For Catawba wine*
> *Has need of no sign,*
> *No tavern-bush to proclaim it.*

⤙ *20 to 30 servings*

INGREDIENTS

7½ OUNCES CANNED PEACHES
(HALF OF A 15-OUNCE CAN)
10 OUNCES CANNED PINEAPPLE CHUNKS
(HALF OF A 20-OUNCE CAN)
3 ORANGES, SLICED
3 LEMONS, SLICED
3 750-ML BOTTLES CATAWBA OR OTHER
SWEET WINE
2 CUPS BRANDY
½ CUP DARK RUM
¼ CUP PLUS 2 TABLESPOONS GREEN
CHARTREUSE

1. In a large mixing bowl, lightly muddle the peaches, pineapple, oranges, and lemons with a wooden spoon. While stirring, slowly add the sweet wine, brandy, rum, and Chartreuse.

2. Transfer the bowl to the refrigerator and chill for at least 6 hours.

3. Place a large block of ice in a punch bowl. Strain the mixture over the ice and serve.

SAUTERNE CUP

From Jerry Thomas' Bartenders Guide: How to Mix Drinks, *1862*

SAUTERNES, A SWEET DESSERT WINE, makes a delightful base for this very refreshing punch. Made with a mixture of lemons, maraschino liqueur, and mint, this bright-tasting, light-colored punch makes a perfect spring or summer drink.

10 to 15 servings

INGREDIENTS

1 750-ML BOTTLE SAUTERNES

½ CUP SIMPLE SYRUP (SEE PAGE 33)

½ CUP LEMON JUICE (ABOUT 3 LEMONS)

1 TABLESPOON MARASCHINO LIQUEUR

1 QUART SELTZER WATER

BUNCH FRESH MINT (ABOUT 10 SPRIGS)

1. In a large pitcher, combine the Sauternes, simple syrup, lemon juice, and maraschino liqueur.

2. Slowly add the seltzer, stirring gently. Garnish cups with the mint.

6.

CHAMPAGNE PUNCHES

"I only drink Champagne when I'm happy, and when I'm sad.
Sometimes I drink it when I'm alone. When I have company,
I consider it obligatory. I trifle with it if I am not hungry and drink
it when I am. Otherwise I never touch it—unless I'm thirsty."

—LILY BOLLINGER, 1894–1977

LIGHT GUARD PUNCH

From Jerry Thomas' Bartenders Guide: How to Mix Drinks, *1862*

As the name of this punch suggests, it is the perfect warm-weather punch for any small regiment (whether military or otherwise). If sherry doesn't appeal, substitute a sweet sparkling wine for a lighter taste.

24 to 36 servings

INGREDIENTS

1 750-ML BOTTLE PALE SHERRY
1 750-ML BOTTLE COGNAC
1 750-ML BOTTLE SAUTERNES
1 PINEAPPLE, PEELED, CORED, AND
  CHOPPED
3 750-ML BOTTLES CHAMPAGNE
4 LEMONS, SLICED

1. Combine the sherry, cognac, Sauternes, and pineapple in a large mixing bowl. Transfer the bowl to the refrigerator and chill for at least 2 hours.

2. To serve, pour the mixture into a punch bowl over a large block of ice, and add the Champagne. Stir gently, and garnish with the lemon slices.

Page 137: THERESIENTHAL CRANBERRY FOOTED PUNCH BOWL (c. 1920), *hand-blown crystal with optic swirl decoration and applied clear foot, Germany*

SPICED PLUM PUNCH

From David Fritzler, Tryst, Washington, D.C.

THIS DRINK PAIRS WARMING SPICES with fresh plums and sparkling wine, making it an attractive red punch for fall. It's great as a light punch for brunch if you omit the port and substitute a light rhum agricole for the aged rum. This Champagne punch actually works with an assortment of spirits, so try what you like. The plum mixture can also easily be blended with sparkling water or cider instead of spirits for a nonalcoholic drink. It can even be combined with a little rum or port and served over ice cream.

The spiced plums need to sit in the syrup for at least twenty-four hours. Three to four days is even better. Whether you are brewing tea or coffee or infusing fruit or alcohol never forget the three "Ts": time, temperature, and turbulence (stirring or shaking). The more you use of each, the more infusion will take place.

~ 18 to 26 servings

INGREDIENTS
1 BLOCK OF ICE
  SPICED PLUMS IN SYRUP (RECIPE FOLLOWS)
3 CUPS AGED RUM SUCH AS FLOR DE
  CAÑA 7 YEAR OR EL DORADO 12 YEAR
2 CUPS RUBY PORT
2½ CUPS APPLE CIDER
½ CUP UNSWEETENED CRANBERRY JUICE
1 750-ML BOTTLE CAVA
  SPRIGS MINT FOR GARNISH

INGREDIENTS FOR SPICED PLUMS
4 CINNAMON STICKS
3 1-INCH CHUNKS OF FRESH GINGER,
  CRUSHED
1 TEASPOON WHOLE CLOVES
1 TEASPOON WHOLE BLACK PEPPER CORNS
2 CUPS DEMERARA SUGAR
1 CUP WATER
1 TEASPOON VANILLA EXTRACT
  APPROXIMATELY 12 MODERATELY
  RIPE, FIRM RED PLUMS

1. Add each ingredient (except for the mint), in order, to the punch bowl. Stir gently and ladle the punch over the ice.

2. Serve with plum slices in each cup, and have bar picks available for those who want to dig them out to eat. Garnish the cups with mint.

For the Spiced Plums

1. Bring the spices, sugar, and water to boil in a medium sauce pan, then reduce the heat to medium-low, and simmer for 15 minutes. Slice 12 plums while the syrup cooks.

2. Remove the syrup from the heat and add the vanilla extract. Place the plums in a heat-safe container and pour the hot syrup over the plums, through a fine mesh strainer.

3. Cool the mixture completely, and then transfer it to a storage container.

BOMBAY PUNCH

From The Ideal Bartender, *1917*

THIS PUNCH is not to be confused with the Bombay Government Regulation Punch of 1694, which is a beefier sailor's drink due to the inclusion of rum. Here the sweet ingredients and lighter alcoholic components make a delightful landlubber's punch characterized by fruit-driven flavors and the sparkle of Champagne.

⌒ *20 to 30 servings*

INGREDIENTS

ZEST OF 3 LEMONS

1¼ CUP DEMERARA SUGAR

½ PINEAPPLE, PEELED, CORED, AND FINELY CHOPPED

3 ORANGES, SLICED

1 LEMON, SLICED

½ PINT STRAWBERRIES, HULLED AND SLICED

2 CUPS BRANDY

2 CUPS SHERRY

2 CUPS MADEIRA

2 750-ML BOTTLES CHAMPAGNE

1 QUART SELTZER WATER

1. In a large mixing bowl, muddle the lemon zest and the sugar with a wooden spoon. Add the pineapple, orange and lemon slices, and strawberries, and continue to muddle lightly.

2. Pour in the brandy, sherry, and Madeira, and stir. The mixture can remain at room temperature for at least 2 hours until you are ready to serve it. The longer it rests, the more the fruit will macerate.

3. To serve, pour the mixture over a large block of ice that has been set in a large punch bowl. Add the Champagne and seltzer water. Stir gently.

LA PATRIA PUNCH

From Jerry Thomas' Bartenders Guide: How to Mix Drinks, *1862*

ALCOHOL IS AN EFFECTIVE SOLVENT capable of quickly releasing the flavors from any fruit soaking in it. This punch calls for a relatively quick infusion with pineapple and oranges, but you can always produce a deeper, more integrated flavor by allowing the fruit to soak in the alcohol longer—even overnight, if you seal and refrigerate the container into which you place the ingredients.

35 to 50 servings

INGREDIENTS

4 ORANGES, SLICED
1 PINEAPPLE, PEELED, CORED, AND SLICED
1 750-ML BOTTLE COGNAC
3 750-ML BOTTLES CHAMPAGNE, CHILLED

1. Place the orange and pineapple slices in a medium mixing bowl and pour the cognac over it. Let the mixture steep unrefrigerated for 2 hours.

2. Pour the macerated fruit and cognac mixture into a punch bowl filled with ice cubes. Pour the Champagne into the punch bowl, stir gently, and serve immediately.

CHAMPAGNE PUNCH

From Practical Recipes, *1909*

⸻ ᏆᎯᏝᎽ ⸻

THIS IS A CLASSIC PUNCH, but just a few variations can help elevate it. When using green tea, Sencha is a particularly good choice. It has a grassy flavor and a nice touch of bitterness. Maraschino cherries are widely available, and recommended for this drink, but if fresh cherries are in season, by all means consider pitting a cup or two of the luscious red fruit and deploying them in the bowl instead.

⁓ *15 to 20 servings*

INGREDIENTS

- 10 OUNCES CANNED PINEAPPLE CHUNKS (HALF OF A 20-OUNCE CAN)
- 1 CUP SIMPLE SYRUP (SEE PAGE 33)
- 2 CUPS WATER, HEATED TO 150 TO 160°F
- 1 GREEN TEA BAG
- ½ 750-ML BOTTLE BRANDY
- ½ 750-ML BOTTLE LIGHT RUM
- ¼ CUP MARASCHINO CHERRIES
- ½ CUP LEMON JUICE (ABOUT 3 LEMONS)
- 2½ CUPS SELTZER WATER
- 2½ CUPS CHAMPAGNE

1. Drain the juice from the pineapple chunks into a medium saucepan, and add the simple syrup. Put the pan over medium heat, and bring the mixture to a boil.

2. Meanwhile, pour the boiling water into a bowl, and add the tea bag. Let it steep until strong, about 10 to 15 minutes. Remove the tea bag, and let the brewed tea cool, about 20 minutes.

3. Add the pineapple simple syrup, rum, and brandy to the cooled tea. Add the lemon juice, cherries, and pineapple chunks. Stir well, transfer the bowl to the refrigerator, and chill for at least 5 hours.

4. To serve, pour the mixture into a punch bowl, and slowly stir while adding the seltzer water and Champagne.

THE MR. & MRS. SYBERT
COMMEMORATIVE PUNCH

From Adam Bernbach, Proof and Estadio, Washington, D.C.

ADAM BERNBACH should get an award from Spain's viticultural industry for creating this punch. It's like a guided tour of great but underappreciated things Spanish vintners do with grapes. Sherry, Cava, and Brandy de Jerez may rarely get the recognition that the products of their flashier EU neighbors do, but they very often deliver loads of flavor, and just as much fun, for your euro or dollar.

~ 20 to 30 servings

INGREDIENTS

3¼ CUPS ORANGE AND THYME SYRUP
    (RECIPE FOLLOWS)
1 750-ML BOTTLE OLOROSO SHERRY
1 750-ML BOTTLE CAVA
2¼ CUPS BRANDY DE JEREZ
1 CUP LIME JUICE (ABOUT 8 LIMES),
    RINDS RESERVED
    STRIPS OF ZEST FROM 2 ORANGES
1 BUNCH OF MINT

INGREDIENTS FOR ORANGE AND
THYME SYRUP
1½ CUPS WATER
    ZEST OF 1 ORANGE
5 SPRIGS OF THYME
3¾ CUPS DEMERARA SUGAR

1. Pour all the liquids into a bowl. Add the lime rinds. Stir.

2. Add a large block of ice to the bowl. Garnish with orange zest and mint sprigs.

For the Orange and Thyme Syrup
1. Heat the water to a boil and pour over the orange zest, thyme, and demerara sugar in a separate bowl. Let sit for 1 hour.

2. Strain the resulting infusion into a glass jar with tight-fitting lid.

REGENT'S PUNCH

From The Dessert Book, *1872*

꧁꧂

REGENT'S PUNCH is named after England's King George IV, known as the Prince Regent in the period from 1811 until his ascension to the throne in 1820. Known more for his drinking and carousing than for his attention to matters of state, the Prince Regent had extravagant tastes and was despised by his subjects as a profligate—which makes him *exactly* the kind of person to trust, at least when it comes to punch.

꧁ 16 to 24 servings

INGREDIENTS

2 GREEN TEA BAGS
3 CUPS WATER, HEATED TO 150 TO 160°F
½ CUP DEMERARA SUGAR
½ 750-ML BOTTLE DRY SHERRY
2 CUPS BRANDY
1 750-ML BOTTLE CHAMPAGNE
1 LEMON, SLICED

1. Put the tea bags in the boiling water and steep for 5 minutes. Remove the tea bags. Add the sugar to the hot tea, stirring until it dissolves, and then allow it to cool.

2. Once the tea is cool, add the sherry and brandy, stirring constantly. Put the bowl in the refrigerator for at least 1 hour.

3. Just before serving, pour the mixture into a punch bowl, add the Champagne, and garnish with the lemon slices.

HANS PUNCH UP

From Adam Bernbach, Proof and Estadio, Washington, D.C.

THE NAME OF THIS RECIPE reminds us that there is more than one way to serve a punch. Generally, "up" for a cocktail means chilled and served in a stemmed glass. So why not drink punch like it is a martini? Nowadays we are conditioned to think punch should be presented in a little glass cup with an even smaller handle, but it was most often consumed in its heyday out of something more like a small wine glass. Instead of adding ice to the glass as suggested here, consider chilling the punch in a bowl with a large ice block and serving it in small, chilled martini glasses.

~ 8 to 12 servings

INGREDIENTS

  2 CUPS PEAR EAU DE VIE OR POIRE
    WILLIAMS BRANDY
  2 CUPS HONEY SYRUP (RECIPE FOLLOWS)
  1 CUP LEMON JUICE (ABOUT 6 LEMONS)
  8 DASHES ANGOSTURA BITTERS
    ICE
  1 CUP SPARKLING WINE
  8 MINT SPRIGS, FOR GARNISH

INGREDIENTS FOR HONEY SYRUP

  1 CUP WATER
  2 CUPS HONEY

1. Combine the pear eau de vie or Poire Williams brandy, honey syrup, lemon juice, and bitters in a punch bowl. Add about a cup of ice, and stir vigorously.

2. To serve, fill 8 highball glasses with ice, divide the punch among the glasses, and top each one with a splash of sparkling wine or Champagne. Stir gently, and garnish each with a mint sprig.

For the Honey Syrup

1. Combine water and honey in a medium saucepan over medium-high heat. Bring to a boil, stirring until the honey has dissolved. Reduce the heat to medium-low, and cook for 5 minutes.

2. Cool completely before using or storing in the refrigerator in a tightly sealed glass jar, where it will keep for 2 to 4 weeks.

THERESIENTHAL CRANBERRY FOOTED PUNCH BOWL ~ CIRCA 1920
Hand-blown crystal with optic swirl decoration and applied clear foot, Germany

7.

MILK PUNCHES

*"Poppea, wife of Domitius Nero, took
five hundred nursing asses everywhere in her traveling party,
and soaked herself completely in a bath of this milk,
in the belief that it would make her skin more supple."*

—PLINY THE ELDER

VICTORIA MILK PUNCH

From Jerry Thomas' Bartenders Guide: How to Mix Drinks, *1862*

MILK PUNCHES have a wonderful creamy texture but can be challenging for the neophyte milk punch maker. Especially when the instructions call for the combination of citrus and milk—a combination most cooks are taught to avoid. Do not worry, simply skim any solids that form before you serve.

35 to 50 servings

INGREDIENTS

2 750-ML BOTTLES BRANDY

2 750-ML BOTTLES DARK JAMAICA RUM

6 LEMONS, SLICED

2 CUPS DEMERARA SUGAR

2 CUPS WHOLE MILK

1¾ QUARTS WATER

1. In a large container with a lid, combine the brandy, rum, and lemons slices. Let the mixture steep at room temperature for at least 24 hours.

2. In a pot, bring the milk to a gentle boil, between 200°F and 212°F, stirring regularly.

3. Add the sugar, milk, and water, stirring gently.

4. Strain the punch through a fine sieve into a large punch bowl. Discard the solids. The punch can be heated in a large pot over medium heat and served warm, or poured over ice.

Page 151: OLD PARIS HARD PASTE PORCELAIN SHADED ROSE DU BARRY (c. 1870s), *hand-painted raised enamel polychrome floral decoration*

AGAVE CON LECHE

From Owen Thompson, Café Atlantico, Washington, D.C.

IN CONTRAST to its forbears made with lemon juice, which allowed them to keep quite a while without spoiling, this punch cannot be stored for long. It's not the milk that will turn the party sour, however; the fresh lime juice is the culprit. It spoils quickly.

16 to 24 servings

INGREDIENTS

2 ⅛ CUPS WHOLE MILK
1 ⅔ CUPS GRAPEFRUIT JUICE, FRESHLY
    SQUEEZED (ABOUT 3 GRAPEFRUIT)
  ½ CUP LIME JUICE (ABOUT 4 LIMES)
  1 750-ML BOTTLE BLANCO TEQUILA
1 ⅔ CUPS ST. GERMAIN ELDERFLOWER
    LIQUEUR

1. In a double boiler, warm the milk to about 120°F, stirring regularly.

2. Combine with juices, and allow the mixture to sit for 15 to 20 minutes. The citrus and milk mixture will curdle during this time.

3. Strain out the curds by first using a large mesh strainer, then by pouring the mixture through coffee filters. This process will result in an almost-clear liquid, which is a mix of citrus and whey.

4. Combine the citrus and whey blend with the tequila and St. Germain, and refrigerate. When ready to serve, pour over a large ice block set in a punch bowl.

NECTAR PUNCH

From Jerry Thomas' Bartenders Guide: How to Mix Drinks, *1862*

THE COMBINATION OF RUM, MILK, AND NUTMEG lends this punch its ambrosial quality, but the addition of zesty citrus is what makes it such a consummate crowd pleaser. Benjamin Franklin enjoyed a similar punch made with brandy and shared his recipe with James Bowdoin, a Massachusetts politician, in a letter from 1763.

40 to 60 servings

INGREDIENTS

2½ CUPS LEMON JUICE (ABOUT 15 LEMONS), RINDS RESERVED

2 1-L BOTTLES DARK RUM

2 QUARTS WHOLE MILK

2 QUARTS COLD WATER

1 TEASPOON FRESHLY GRATED NUTMEG

5 CUPS FINE DEMERARA SUGAR

1. Cut the rinds from the lemons into thin strips and soak them for 8 hours in the rum.

2. In a pot, bring the milk to a gentle boil, between 200°F and 212°F, stirring regularly.

3. Add the lemon juice to the infused rum. Add the milk, water, and nutmeg. Cover the bowl, and let the mixture stand for 24 hours in the refrigerator.

4. Add the sugar and stir until dissolved. To serve, strain the punch through a fine sieve into a large punch bowl filled with ice.

HAND-BLOWN WHITE-COVERED BRISTOL GLASS "TOM & JERRY" SET ~ CIRCA 1870
Hand-painted raised enamel decoration, English

KREMAS A NEW WHEY

From Owen Thompson, Café Atlantico, Washington, D.C.

=== ⌒⟲⟲⟲⟲ ===

NAMED FOR KREMAS, a traditional Haitian milk punch made with sweet canned milk, this new punch uses an old-fashioned punch-making technique, and pays further homage to old-style punches by using a traditional Haitian rum. Rhum Barbancourt's Cognac-inspired distillery was modernized over fifty years ago, but the rum is still made from pressed cane juice, not molasses as most rums are. The resulting flavor is just as it was in the 1860s, when production began.

⌒ 16 to 24 servings

INGREDIENTS

2 ¼ CUPS WHOLE MILK

1 ⅔ CUPS GRAPEFRUIT JUICE, FRESHLY SQUEEZED (ABOUT 3 GRAPEFRUIT)

½ CUP LIME JUICE (ABOUT 4 LIMES)

1 750-ML BOTTLE RHUM BARBANCOURT 3- OR 5-STAR

1 ⅔ CUPS TAYLOR'S VELVET FALERNUM OR HOMEMADE FALERNUM SYRUP (SEE PAGE 35)

1 LARGE ICE BLOCK

1. In a double boiler, warm the milk to 120°F, stirring regularly.

2. Combine the warm milk with the juices and allow the mixture to sit for 15 to 20 minutes. The citrus and milk will curdle while it rests.

3. First strain out the curds by using a large mesh strainer, and then pour the liquid through coffee filters. This process will result in an almost-clear liquid, which is a mix of citrus and whey.

4. Combine the citrus and whey mixture with the rum and falernum. Refrigerate the punch.

5. When ready to serve, pour the punch over a large ice block set in a punch bowl.

CAMBRIDGE MILK PUNCH

From Cooling Cups and Dainty Drinks, *1869*

THE ORIGINAL VERSION of this delicious punch presents a major challenge to the home mixologist—bitter almonds are almost impossible to come by because they contain a chemical that transforms into cyanide in the presence of water. Add dashes of pure almond extract (which is made from bitter almonds) in small doses to boost the flavor.

~ *15 to 20 servings*

INGREDIENTS

- 2 QUARTS WHOLE MILK
- 12 LIGHTLY CRUSHED SWEET ALMONDS
- ¼ TEASPOON PURE ALMOND EXTRACT
  ZEST OF 2 LEMONS
- 1¼ CUPS DEMERARA SUGAR
- 3 EGG WHITES
- 2 TABLESPOONS WHOLE MILK, COLD
- 2 CUPS BRANDY
- 1 CUP DARK RUM

1. In a large saucepan set over medium heat, combine the milk, almonds, almond extract, lemon zest, and sugar. Bring the mixture to a gentle boil, between 200°F and 212°F, stirring regularly, and cook for about 5 minutes. Strain the milk, discarding the solids, and keep the liquid warm.

2. Whisk the egg whites with several tablespoons of cold milk and stir them into the warm milk mixture. While stirring, add the brandy and rum. Beat the mixture vigorously until it has a light froth on top.

3. Pour into a punch bowl, and serve immediately.

A NOTE ABOUT USING EGGS: Using raw eggs in any recipe carries with it the remote possibility of causing illness. If you decide to make a punch recipe that calls for raw eggs or raw egg whites, make sure to find the freshest eggs possible (check the date on the carton if you're not using farm-fresh eggs), and wash and rinse the outside of the eggs carefully before cracking them open. Always proceed with caution and let your guests (especially those who are elderly or pregnant) know you have used raw eggs in the preparation of the punch.

DOULTON BURSLEM AESTHETIC MOVEMENT TALL FOOTED PUNCH BOWL ~ CIRCA 1890
Brown transfer decoration and hand-painted highlights of pink and yellow

CALIFORNIA MILK PUNCH

From Jerry Thomas' Bartenders Guide: How to Mix Drinks, *1862*

THIS VERSION of the popular California Milk Punch is not for the labor averse: it contains a lot of ingredients and is complicated to prepare. Of course, the complex, intriguing punch that results is well worth the effort, and anyone who takes the time to make it will understand why the recipe is so revered.

~ 20 to 30 servings

INGREDIENTS

- 3 CUPS WATER, HEATED TO 150 TO 160°F
- 1 GREEN TEA BAG
- ½ PINEAPPLE, PEELED, CORED, AND SLICED
- ⅔ CUP LEMON JUICE (ABOUT 4 LEMONS)
- ZEST OF 1 LEMON
- ½ CUP DEMERARA SUGAR, DISSOLVED IN 2 CUPS HOT WATER
- 10 CORIANDER SEEDS
- 3 WHOLE CLOVES
- 1 750-ML BOTTLE CATAWBA, TOKAJI, OR OTHER SWEET WINE
- 1 CUP BRANDY
- 1 CUP DARK JAMAICA RUM
- ½ CUP BATAVIA ARRACK
- 2 CUPS WHOLE MILK

1. Combine 1 cup of the hot water and the tea bag in a bowl and steep for at least 5 minutes. Remove the tea bag.

2. Using a wooden spoon, muddle together the pineapple, ⅓ cup lemon juice, lemon zest, sugar, coriander, and cloves in a large bowl. Slowly add the sweet wine, brandy, rum, and arrack, stirring constantly. Add the tea and the remaining 2 cups of hot water. Cover the bowl tightly and allow it to rest for at least 6 hours.

3. In a separate pot, bring the milk to a gentle boil, between 200°F and 212°F.

4. Uncover the bowl and add the hot milk and the remaining lemon juice. Stir well and filter through a cheesecloth at least two times to remove all solids.

5. When the punch is clear, pour into a large punch bowl that has been filled with ice, and serve.

BANNISTER'S MILK PUNCH

From Cooling Cups and Dainty Drinks, *1869*

LIKE ALL MILK PUNCHES OF THE TIME, the original recipe for Bannister's Milk Punch calls for the punch maker to scald the milk, which meant heating it to around 185°F while stirring relentlessly. Back then, scalding was used to achieve two basic goals: first, to kill any harmful bacteria; and second, to denature the proteins and thin the milk. Today, milk is pasteurized so bacteria are of less concern, though the milk still needs to be heated.

~ *24 to 36 servings*

INGREDIENTS

2 CUPS DARK RUM
9 LEMONS, THINLY SLICED
6 CUPS WATER
1 750-ML BOTTLE BRANDY
1¼ CUPS ORANGE JUICE, FRESHLY
    SQUEEZED (ABOUT 5 ORANGES)
¾ CUP LEMON JUICE (ABOUT 5 LEMONS)
3 CUPS DEMERARA SUGAR
1 QUART WHOLE MILK
1 TABLESPOON FRESHLY GRATED NUTMEG

1. At least 3 days before you plan to serve the punch, combine the rum and lemon slices in a large bowl. Cover the bowl tightly, and let steep in the refrigerator.

2. Heat the milk to 185°F, stirring regularly. To make the punch, add the water, brandy, orange and lemon juices, and sugar to the infused rum. Add the milk and nutmeg, stir well, and cover the bowl again. Transfer the bowl to the refrigerator, and let the mixture chill for 2 hours.

3. Strain the punch through cheesecloth or a sieve into a large punch bowl that has been filled with ice. Let the punch sit for at least 20 minutes before serving.

8.

TEA PUNCHES

"Thank God for tea! What would the world do without tea! How did it exist? I am glad I was not born before tea."

—SIR PHILIP SIDNEY,
English statesman, 1554–1586

GREEN TEA PUNCH

From Cups and Their Customs, *1869*

═══════════════ ⌀⌀⌀ ═══════════════

ERRING ON THE SIDE OF CAUTION is the key to making and serving this punch. Placing a flaming glass of punch into the hands of your guests makes for a wonderful spectacle, but the drinkers need to be warned clearly that they must blow out the flame before tasting the contents of their glasses.

8 to 12 servings

INGREDIENTS

1 QUART WATER, HEATED TO 150 TO 160°F
1 GREEN TEA BAG
1 CUP BRANDY
1 CUP DARK RUM
½ CUP DEMERARA SUGAR, DISSOLVED
   IN 1½ CUPS WATER
5 CUBES HARD SUGAR
3 TABLESPOONS LEMON JUICE
   (ABOUT 1 LEMON), RIND RESERVED
MATCHES

1. Combine the hot water and tea bag in a large bowl, and steep for 5 minutes. Discard the tea bag.

2. Bring water to a boil in the bottom of a double boiler and set the top half in the bottom. When the top half is hot, add the brandy, rum, sugar and water mixture, and lemon juice. Stir until well blended, and add it to the punch bowl. Using a wooden spoon, muddle the zest of the lemon and the cubes of sugar, and add them to the punch bowl.

3. Carefully light the contents of the bowl on fire. While the punch is still flaming, slowly pour in the green tea and stir with a metal ladle.

4. Ladle the punch into individual glasses and have the imbiber blow the flame out before drinking!

Page 165: OLD PARIS HARD PASTE PORCELAIN SHADED ROSE DU BARRY (c. 1870s), *hand-painted raised enamel polychrome floral decoration*

TCHOUPITOULAS PUNCH

From The Bon Vivants, San Francisco, California

THE BON VIVANTS, aka cocktail consultants Scott Baird and Josh Harris, attended Tales of the Cocktail in post-Katrina New Orleans, arriving a little early in order to join other bartenders in a day of volunteering for Hands on New Orleans. While there, they helped build Frederick Douglass High School, a KIPP Charter School. The Bon Vivants were so impressed by the experience they decided to redirect the proceeds from one of their own events to benefit the school. This community-minded spirit is commemorated in this delicious punch, named for a famous street in New Orleans.

15 to 20 servings

INGREDIENTS

1 750-ML BOTTLE WILD TURKEY 101 BOURBON
½ CUP BENEDICTINE
1⅔ CUPS NOILLY PRAT SWEET VERMOUTH
1½ CUPS ORANGE JUICE, FRESHLY SQUEEZED (ABOUT 6 ORANGES)
1½ CUPS LEMON JUICE (ABOUT 9 LEMONS)
2 CUPS EARL GREY TEA (DENSELY BREWED TO TASTE, AND COOLED)
½ CUP RICH SIMPLE SYRUP (RECIPE FOLLOWS)
1 TEASPOON PEYCHAUD'S BITTERS, ABOUT 50 DASHES
1 LARGE ICE BLOCK
3 PEACHES OR ½ PINEAPPLE, SLICED

INGREDIENTS FOR RICH SIMPLE SYRUP

½ CUP WATER
1 CUP ORGANIC EVAPORATED CANE SUGAR

1. Combine the ingredients in a large bowl, add the ice block, and stir.

2. Garnish the cups with sliced fresh peaches or fresh pineapple.

For the Rich Simple Syrup
1. Boil water, stir in cane sugar, and simmer on low heat for 5 minutes, skimming any foam that appears.

2. Let the mixture cool before using.

OLD PARIS HARD PASTE PORCELAIN SHADED ROSE DU BARRY ~ CIRCA 1870S
Hand-painted raised enamel polychrome floral decoration

ST. CECILIA PUNCH

~ Circa 1900 ~

THE ST. CECILIA SOCIETY was founded in the eighteenth century in Charleston, South Carolina, as a private concert organization in honor of St. Cecilia, the patron saint of music. Today, it remains an exclusive society for elite descendants of Charleston's "aristocracy," though it no longer stages concerts as it once did. If you find the recipe too sweet, try substituting additional brandy for the peach brandy.

~ 24 to 36 servings

INGREDIENTS

2 CUPS BRANDY
1½ LEMONS, SLICED
2 CUPS BREWED GREEN TEA
2 CUPS PEACH BRANDY
1 CUP DARK RUM
1¾ CUPS DEMERARA SUGAR
½ PINEAPPLE, PEELED, CORED, AND SLICED
2 750-ML BOTTLES CHAMPAGNE, CHILLED
1 QUART SELTZER WATER

1. In a small bowl, combine the brandy and lemon slices. Steep for at least 24 hours.

2. Add the tea, peach brandy, rum, sugar, and pineapple slices to the mixture. Stir well.

3. Pour it into a punch bowl that has been filled with ice cubes. Add the Champagne and seltzer, stirring gently. Serve immediately.

CAULDON ENGLAND AESTHETIC MOVEMENT LOW PUNCH BOWL ~ CIRCA 1890

Transfer design depicting hibiscus flowers with gold trim
and hand-painted with polychrome enamel decoration

ZOAR VALLEY PUNCH

From Chantal Tseng, The Tabard Inn, Washington, D.C.

A COMMON TECHNIQUE to make a more flavorful punch is to substitute tea, green or black, for any water a recipe calls for. Here, the water used to dilute the maple syrup so it will dissolve easily in the punch is actually brewed tea.

12 to 18 servings

INGREDIENTS

1¼ CUPS LIME JUICE (ABOUT 10 LIMES)
2½ CUPS ORANGE JUICE, FRESHLY
　　SQUEEZED (ABOUT 10 ORANGES)
　　BLACK TEA MAPLE SYRUP TO TASTE
　　(RECIPE FOLLOWS)
¼ CUP ST. ELIZABETH ALLSPICE DRAM
1 750-ML BOTTLE LAIRD'S BONDED APPLE
　　BRANDY OR OTHER APPLE BRANDY
1 750-ML BOTTLE OF DARK RUM
　　(PREFERABLY JAMAICAN)
1 LARGE ICE BLOCK
2 LIMES, SLICED
2 ORANGES, SLICED
　　FRESHLY GRATED NUTMEG

INGREDIENTS FOR BLACK TEA
MAPLE SYRUP

2 CUPS BLACK TEA
1 CUP MAPLE SYRUP

1. In a large punch bowl, stir together the first 6 ingredients. Add the ice block 15 minutes before serving. Float the lime and orange slices in the bowl.

2. Grate fresh nutmeg over each glass of punch before serving.

For the Black Tea Maple Syrup

1. Brew black tea (don't steep more than 4 minutes). Remove or discard the tea bags or loose tea.

2. Add maple syrup, and stir. Strain through a fine mesh sieve into a glass jar with tight-fitting lid, and refrigerate until ready to use.

OTRANTO CLUB PUNCH

~ Circa 1890 ~

THIS RECIPE comes from the famous Charleston Receipts and is an homage to the famous club in Charleston, South Carolina. This punch reflects a genteel approach to punch making from a bygone era of the old South.

18 to 26 servings

INGREDIENTS

2 CUPS WATER, HEATED TO 150 TO 160°F
1 GREEN TEA BAG
1¼ CUPS DEMERARA SUGAR
1 1-L BOTTLE BRANDY OR RYE WHISKEY
2 CUPS DARK RUM
1 CUP PEACH BRANDY
1 CUP LEMON JUICE (ABOUT 6 LEMONS)
1 QUART SELTZER WATER
3 LEMONS, THINLY SLICED

1. In a large bowl, combine the water and tea bag. Steep for at least 5 minutes. Remove the tea bag and add the sugar, stirring until dissolved. Add the brandy, rum, peach brandy, and lemon juice.

2. Stir well, and pour the mixture into a large punch bowl that has been filled with ice. Add the seltzer, and stir gently. Serve the punch in small glasses; garnish with the lemon slices.

FROST PUNCH

Adapted from Trader Vic's Book of Food & Drink, *1946*

"Curaçao" is a generic term for orange-flavored liqueur, although it does generally specify sour oranges and sometimes the addition of brandy. Avoid cheap "triple-sec," anything blue, and overly sweet orange liqueurs, because the quality of this distinctive liqueur will dramatically affect the taste of your punch.

24 to 36 servings

INGREDIENTS

1 CUP STRONG GREEN TEA
   RINDS OF 2 LEMONS, THINLY SLICED
1 CUP LEMON JUICE (ABOUT 6 LEMONS)
½ PINEAPPLE, PEELED, CORED,
   AND THINLY SLICED
1 CUP DEMERARA SUGAR
1 CUP BRANDY
¾ CUP CURAÇAO OR OTHER ORANGE
   LIQUEUR
½ CUP DARK RUM
2 CUPS SELTZER WATER
1 750-ML BOTTLE CHAMPAGNE, CHILLED

1. Put the lemon rinds in a mixing bowl. Add the lemon juice, sliced pineapple, brandy, orange liqueur, and rum, and stir well. Transfer the bowl to the refrigerator, and chill the mixture for at least 3 hours.

2. To serve, slowly pour the mixture into a punch bowl that has been filled with ice cubes. Gently stir in the seltzer and Champagne, and serve.

G. M. GURTON'S PUNCH

~ Circa 1850 ~

THIS DELICIOUS TEA PUNCH can be made a vibrant green by using blue Curaçao instead of the generally preferred clear variety. If you would like this punch in a less startling hue, use clear Curaçao or another clear orange liqueur to create a pale grass-colored punch that is every bit as delicious.

18 to 26 servings

INGREDIENTS

1 CUP DARK RUM
1 CUP SHERRY
1 CUP BRANDY
½ CUP BLUE CURAÇAO OR OTHER
   ORANGE LIQUEUR
2 CUPS LIME JUICE (ABOUT 16 LIMES)
½ CUP GINGER SYRUP
6 CUPS WEAK GREEN TEA

INGREDIENTS FOR GINGER SYRUP

½ CUP WHITE SUGAR
½ CUP WATER
1 KNOB FRESH GINGER, ROUGHLY
   CHOPPED

1. In a large punch bowl, combine the rum, sherry, brandy, Curaçao, lime juice, and ginger syrup.

2. Add the hot tea, stir well, and sweeten to taste with the simple syrup. Serve immediately.

For Ginger Syrup
1. Follow the instructions for making simple syrup on page 33, adding the ginger as soon as the sugar has dissolved.

2. Allow the syrup to sit for 1 hour before straining through a fine sieve and adding to punch.

PART III

PUNCH RESOURCES

FOR FURTHER READING

While this book provides facts and recipes about the world of punch and punch bowls, there's always more to learn. The subject is rich with fascinating (and occasionally upsetting) information about everything from pirates and pioneering bartenders to the rum trade and the economics and culture of sugar plantations.

And a Bottle of Rum: A History of the New World in Ten Cocktails, by Wayne Curtis

Bury the Chains: Prophets and Rebels in the Fight to Free an Empire's Slaves, by Adam Hochschild

Imbibe! From Absinthe Cocktail to Whiskey Smash, a Salute in Stories and Drinks to "Professor" Jerry Thomas, Pioneer of the American Bar, by David Wondrich

Enslaving Spirits: The Portuguese-Brazilian Alcohol Trade at Luanda and Its Hinterland, C. 1550–1830, by Jose C. Curto

The Pirate Hunter: The True Story of Captain Kidd, by Richard Zacks

The Pirates Laffite: The Treacherous World of the Corsairs of the Gulf, by William C. Davis

Punch: The Delights and Dangers of the Flowing Bowl, by David Wondrich

The Republic of Pirates: Being the True and Surprising Story of the Caribbean Pirates and the Man Who Brought them Down, by Colin Woodard

RESOURCES

The older recipes in this book were compiled from a number of cocktail, drink, and lifestyle books from the nineteenth and early twentieth centuries. Within the pages of these excellent books we also found recipes that pre-date the nineteenth century, so keep your eyes open for those treasures. We also found several websites with valuable punch-related information and have listed them below as well.

Books

The Book of Days: A Miscellany of Popular Antiquities, edited by Robert Chambers, 1832

The Ceramic Art of Great Britain, by Llewellyn Frederick William Jewitt, 1883

Chafing-Dish Recipes, by Gesine Lemcke, 1896

China Collecting in America, by Alice Morse Earle, 1892

Cooling Cups and Dainty Drinks, by William Terrington, 1869

Cups and Their Customs, by George Edwin Roberts and Henry Porter, 1869

The Dessert Book, by A Boston Lady, 1872

Jerry Thomas' Bartenders Guide: How to Mix Drinks, by Jerry Thomas, 1862

Modern American Drinks, by George J. Kappeler, 1895

Practical Recipes, by Mrs. B. B. Cutter, 1909

Stage-Coach and Tavern Days, by Alice Morse Earle, 1900

Trader Vic's Book of Food & Drink, by Victor Bergeron, 1946

Yale Book of American Verse, edited by Thomas R. Lounsbury, 1912

Websites

"Don't Put Away That Punch Bowl Just Yet, Cratchit,"
by Steven Stern, www.nytimes.com

"History of Alcohol in America," www.2020site.org/drinks/punch.html

www.hobsonchoice.com

www.lostpastremembered.blogspot.com

www.ministryofrum.com

"Pisco Punch," www.bunnyhugs.org/2007/12/03/pisco-punch

"Punch Bowls and Punches," www.2020site.org

"Punch Makes a Classic Comeback,"
by Betty Hallock, www.latimes.com

"The Return of Punch: The Big Cocktail in a Bowl Makes a Comeback,"
by Roxanne Webber, www.chow.com/stories/11080

"Rum, Pirates and the Caribbean," www.articlealley.com/article_65845_26.html

"What America's Oldest Club May Quaff,"
by Eric Felten, www.online.wsj.com

PUNCH BAR ESSENTIALS

Anyone who cares to entertain at home will at some point bump up against the necessity of amassing the essential elements of a bar. This includes liquor, mixers, utensils, ice buckets, and the like. For those who wish to include punches in their repertoire, the basic at-home bar needs to be tweaked a little bit. Below is a list of some of the items you may want to have on hand. Fresh fruit and herbs should be purchased as necessary.

Liquors
Applejack or Calvados
Arrack
Bourbon
Brandy
Champagne or other sparkling
   white wine
Dry sherry
London Dry Gin
Madeira
Maraschino liqueur
Orange liqueur
Peach brandy
Red wine
Rye
Rum (dark and light)
Sauternes or other sweet dessert wine
Sweet sherry
Vermouth, sweet and dry
Whiskey
White wine

Other Essentials
Mixers
Black tea
Club soda
Coconut milk
Green tea
Milk
Seltzer

Added Flavorings and Spices
Allspice
Angostura bitters
Canned cherries
Cinnamon sticks
Falernum syrup
Fruit jellies (guava, apple, etc.)
Nutmeg
Orgeat syrup
Sugar (brown, white, powdered,
   and demerara)
Sugar cubes

PUNCH BOWL CATALOG

ELISE ABRAMS began collecting antique porcelain and stemware over thirty years ago and has become the recognized expert in the field. The punch bowls featured throughout this book are from her collection. Her passion for creating magnificent table settings, coupled with her incomparable collections, culminated in the establishment of *Elise Abrams Antiques* in Great Barrington, Massachusetts, in 1989. Specializing in fine antiques for dining, her inventory ranges from one-of-a-kind pieces to entire services. Ms. Abrams' love of punch bowls is evident in her collection, which is an exquisite selection of porcelain and glass in many patterns, shapes, and sizes.

Abrams is the author of *Hand Painted Porcelain Plates*, has made personal appearances on *The Martha Stewart Show,* and has been featured in *Architectural Digest*, *Country Living*, *Departures*, *Victoria*, *House and Garden*, *Martha Stewart Living*, *Food & Wine*, *Colonial Homes*, *Traditional Home*, and *Elle Décor*.

Elise Abrams Antiques exhibits at the International Antiques and Fine Art Fair and the International Palm Beach Jewelry and Antiques Show in Palm Beach, Florida.

page 9 ~ Circa 1890 Pairpoint Silver Plated Ladle *with lobe-shaped bowl and "Aesthetic Movement" repoussé handle with acanthus leaves and floral decoration*

page 9 ~ Circa 1920s Silver Plate Punch Ladle *with elaborately shaped cup and sterling silver handle*

page 9 ~ Circa 1910 Rogers Brother Neo-Classical Silver Plate Punch Ladle *with barley-twist stem and helmet-shaped bowl*

page 9 ~ Circa 1900 J. B. and S. M. Knowles Sterling Silver Art Nouveau Ladle *with elaborate scrolling, lobed bowl with gold wash interior*

pages 165 and 169
Circa 1870s
**Old Paris Hard Paste
Porcelain Shaded
Rose Du Barry**
*hand-painted raised enamel
polychrome floral decoration*

page 118 ~ Circa 1920s
**Pairpoint Hand-Blown
Cobalt Crystal Footed
Grape Juice Bowl**
*copper wheel engraved
"Vintage" pattern*

page 11 ~ Circa 1890
**Lobmeyr Hand-Blown
Crystal Footed and
Covered Punch Bowl**
*with hand-painted, two-color,
raised paste gold grapes and
leaves and matching punch
cups, Austria*

page 12 ~ Circa 1890
**Signed Lobmeyr
Footed Crystal Punch Cup**
*hand-blown with hand-
painted enamel decoration,
Austria*

pages 8 and 160 ~ Circa 1890
**Doulton Burslem
Aesthetic Movement
Tall Footed Punch Bowl**
*brown transfer decoration and
hand-painted highlights of
pink and yellow*

page 25 ~ Circa 1880
**Doulton Burslem
Footed Punch Bowl**
*English ceraminc, blue
and white transfer*

page 28 ~ Circa 1890
**Royal Furnivals
England Rustic Pattern
Footed Punch Bowl**
*frolicking Bacchus transfer
decoration scalloped rim with
luster finish*

page 31 ~ Circa 1920s
**WMF Hand Blown Crystal
Globular Shaped Punch Bowl**
*mounted on silver plate stand
with handles and matching
top, Germany*

page 172 ~ Circa 1890
**Cauldon England Aesthetic
Movement Low Punch Bowl**
*transfer design depicting
hibiscus flowers with gold
trim and hand-painted with
polychrome enamel decoration*

**page 45 ~ Circa 1890
Hand-Blown Crystal
Punch Cup with
Intaglio Wheel Cutting**
*reverse painted with gold
and polychrome enamel
strawberry decoration*

**page 45 ~ Circa 1920s
Signed Heisey American
Molded Crystal Greek
Key Punch Bowl**
*two-part footed large
punch bowl*

**page 45 ~ 19th Century
Two-Part Hand-Blown
Crystal Punch Bowl**
*with wheel cut
"Vintage" pattern*

**page 44 ~ Circa 1940s
Harrach Amethyst Overlay
Cut to Clear Punch Bowl**
with gold overlay, Germany

**pages 49 and 58 ~ Circa 1890
Furnivals England
Footed Punch Bowl**
*Greek transfer decoration,
hand-colored polychrome
enamel decoration with
gold trim*

**page 85 ~ Circa 1880
Doulton Burslem Footed
Porcelain Punch Bowl**
*hand-painted enamel,
Arts and Crafts style floral
decoration in unusual palette
of bittersweet orange and
green with gold tracery*

**page 103 ~ Circa 1910
Royal Doulton Arts and
Crafts Footed Punch Bowl**
*decorated with all-over poppy
transfer decoration
and polychrome enamel*

**pages 69 and 78 ~ Circa 1930s
Wedgewood "Old Vine"
Pattern Diminutive
Punch Bowl**
*transfer and hand-colored
luster decoration*

**pages 87 and 100 ~ Circa 1900
English Arts and Crafts
Porcelain Footed Punch Bowl**
*polychrome enamel decoration
in the William Morris style*

page 93 ~ Circa 1890
**Furnivals Aesthetic
Movement Punch Bowl**
*scalloped rim and all-over
hibiscus floral pattern*

pages 105 and 112 ~ Circa 1920
**Villeroy and Boch
Footed Punch Bowl**
*blue and white transfer
featuring all-over landscapes,
Germany*

pages 121 and 131 ~ Circa 1880
**Doulton Burslem Aesthetic
Movement Punch Bowl**
*all-over two-color blue enamel
ground with "Japonesque"
motif gold overlay*

pages 137 and 149 ~ Circa 1920
**Theresienthal Cranberry
Footed Punch Bowl**
*hand-blown crystal with optic
swirl decoration and
applied clear foot, Germany*

page 151 ~ Circa 1870s
**Old Paris Hard Paste
Porcelain Shaded
Rose Du Barry**
*hand-painted raised enamel
polychrome floral decoration*

pages 17 and 156 ~ Circa 1870
**Hand-Blown White-Covered
Bristol Glass "Tom & Jerry" Set**
*tray with matching punch
cups; hand-painted raised
enamel decoration, England*

INDEX

ABOUT THE AUTHOR

DAN SEARING is a founding member and current vice president of the D.C. Craft Bartenders Guild. In 2009 he hosted Punch Club, a weekly event focusing on classic and contemporary punches with his partners at Room 11, where he is the bar manager. He has contributed punch and cocktail recipes to publications, including *Imbibe* and *Flavor*. This is his first book. He lives in Washington, D.C., with his wife, Kristin, and his daughter, Maggie.

ACKNOWLEDGMENTS

Thanks to all of those who contributed their original punch recipes. A special thanks to Elise Abrams, Helen Clarke, Terry Deal, Laurie Dolphin, Mark A. Gore, Jessica Jones, Nathaniel Marunas, Allison Meierding, Rosy Ngo, Eric Seed, Ken Skalski, and Stuart S. Shapiro.

I would also like to thank Derek Brown and the other founding members of the D.C. Craft Bartenders Guild, especially the Hummingbird to Mars gents; my partners in Room 11, Ben Gilligan, Nick Pimintel, and Paul Ruppert; and my family, in particular my parents and my wife, Kristin.

PHOTOGRAPHY CREDITS

Cocktail photographs on pages 50, 55, 62, 71, 75, 81, 82, 88, 94, 97, 107, 108, 115, 122, 127, 135, 139, 142, 146, 153, 159, 163, 166, 170, 177, and front cover by Ken Skalski © 2011

Punch bowl and ladle photographs on pages 8, 9, 11, 12, 17, 25, 28, 31, 44, 45, 49, 58, 69, 78, 85, 87, 93, 100, 103, 105, 112, 118, 121, 131, 137, 149, 151, 156, 160, 165, 169, and 172 by Stuart S. Shapiro © 2011

Still life photographs on pages 33, 34, 37, 41, and 42 by Mark A. Gore © 2011

page 16, "Detroit, Michigan," 1942; © Arthur S. Siegel. Courtesy of the Library of Congress

page 17, "An Accurate Map of the West Indies," c. 1752; © Emanuel Bowen. Courtesy of the Library of Congress

page 18, "The Catch Singers," 1775; © Guildhall Library & Art Gallery/ StockphotoPro

page 19, "Bringing in the Wassail Bowl," 1874; © Henry Stacy Marks/The Print Collector/StockphotoPro

page 21, "Economy," 1816; © George Cruikshank. Courtesy of the Library of Congress

page 23, "View of a Skittle Ground at Hampstead," 1813; © Guildhall Library & Art Gallery/StockphotoPro

page 27 and back cover, "Anacreontick's in Full Song," 1801; © James Gillray. Courtesy of the Library of Congress

Endpapers, "West Indies Map," c. 1750s; © Emanuel Bowen. Courtesy of the Library of Congress

MARK A. GORE has photographed many book projects. He also shoots live music, mostly punk rock. He lives in Brooklyn with his wife and daughter and can be reached at mag_foto@me.com.

STUART S. SHAPIRO is a filmmaker and photographer and is best known for *Night Flight*, his award winning series on USA Network. The president and founder of iConstituent in Washington D.C., he is an innovator of Congressional constituent communications. He is married to Laurie Dolphin.

KEN SKALSKI is a New York–based commercial still-life photographer with a degree from Rochester Institute of Technology and more than thirty years of experience. His clients range from Fortune 500 companies to small Internet start-ups, and his work appears in numerous national publications, as well as specialty corporate magazines and catalogs. Ken currently lives with his family in Ossining, New York.

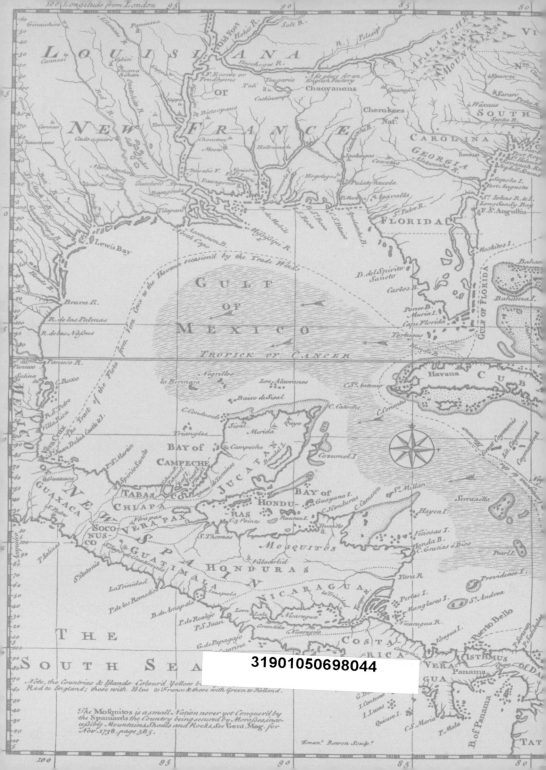